Read On . . . Sports

Read On . . . Sports

Reading Lists for Every Taste

Craig A. Clark and Richard T. Fox

Read On Series
Barry Trott, Series Editor

 LIBRARIES UNLIMITED

AN IMPRINT OF ABC-CLIO, LLC
Santa Barbara, California • Denver, Colorado • Oxford, England

Library of Congress Cataloging-in-Publication Data

Clark, Craig A.
  Read on . . . sports : reading lists for every taste / Craig Clark, Richard T. Fox.
    pages cm. — (Read on series)
    ISBN 978-1-61069-357-8 (pbk.) — ISBN 978-1-61069-358-5 (ebook)
1. Sports—Bibliography. I. Title.
  Z7511.C53 2014
  016.796—dc23   2013034587

ISBN: 978-1-61069-357-8
EISBN: 978-1-61069-358-5

18 17 16 15 14   1 2 3 4 5

This book is also available on the World Wide Web as an eBook.
Visit www.abc-clio.com for details.

Libraries Unlimited
An Imprint of ABC-CLIO, LLC

ABC-CLIO, LLC
130 Cremona Drive, P.O. Box 1911
Santa Barbara, California 93116-1911

This book is printed on acid-free paper ∞

Manufactured in the United States of America

Contents

Series Foreword

Welcome to Libraries Unlimited's Read On series of fiction and nonfiction genre guides for readers' advisors and for readers. The Read On series introduces readers and those who work with them to new ways of looking at books, genres, and reading interests.

Over the past decade, readers' advisory services have become vital in public libraries. A quick glance at the schedule of any library conference at the state or national level will reveal a wealth of programs on various aspects of connecting readers to books they will enjoy. Working with unfamiliar genres or types of reading can be a challenge, particularly for those new to the field. Equally, readers may find it a bit overwhelming to look for books outside their favorite authors and preferred reading interests. The titles in the Read On series offer you a new way to approach reading:

- they introduce you a broad sampling of materials available in a given genre;
- they offer you new directions to explore in a genre—through appeal features and unconventional topics;
- they help readers' advisors better understand and navigate genres with which they are less familiar; and
- they provide reading lists that you can use to create quick displays, include on your library websites and in the library newsletter, or to hand out to readers.

The lists in the Read On series are arranged in sections based on appeal characteristics—story, character, setting, and language (as described in Joyce Saricks's *Reader's Advisory Services in the Public Library*, 3d ed., ALA Editions, 2005), with a fifth section on mood. These are hidden elements of a book that attract readers. Remember that a book can have multiple appeal factors; and sometimes readers are drawn to a particular book for several factors, while other times for only one. In the Read On lists, titles are placed according to their primary appeal characteristics, and then put into a list that reflects common reading interests. So if you are working with a reader who loves fantasy that features quests for magical objects or a reader who is interested in memoirs with a strong sense of place you will be able to find a list of titles whose main appeal centers around this search. Each list indicates a title that is an especially good starting place for readers, an exemplar of that appeal characteristic.

Story is perhaps the most basic appeal characteristic. It relates to the plot of the book—What are the elements of the tale? Is the emphasis more on the people or the situations? Is the story action focused or more interior? Is it funny? Scary?

Many readers are drawn to the books they love by the characters. The character appeal reflects such aspects as whether there are lots of characters or only a single main character; Are the characters easily recognizable types? Do the characters grow and change over the course of the story? What are the characters' occupations?

Setting covers a range of elements that might appeal to readers. What is the time period or geographic locale of the tale? How much does the author describe the surroundings of the story? Does the reader feel as though he or she is "there," when reading the book? Are there special features such as the monastic location of Ellis Peters's Brother Cadfael mysteries or the small town setting of Jan Karon's Mitford series?

Although not traditionally considered appeal characteristic, mood is important to readers as well. It relates to how the author uses the tools of narrative—language, pacing, story, and character—to create a feeling for the work. Mood can be difficult to quantify because the reader brings his or her own feelings to the story as well. Mood really asks how does the book make the reader feel? Creepy? Refreshed? Joyful? Sad?

Finally, the language appeal brings together titles where the author's writing style draws the reader. This can be anything from a lyrical prose style with lots of flourishes to a spare use of language à la Hemingway. Humor, snappy dialog, wordplay, recipes, and other language elements all have the potential to attract readers.

Dig into these lists. Use them to find new titles and authors in a genre that you love, or as a guide to expand your knowledge of a new type of writing. . . . Above all, read, enjoy, and remember—never apologize for your reading tastes!

—*Barry Trott*
Series Editor

Acknowledgments

I would like to thank:

My wife Cathy and my daughter Victoria, for letting me sneak out of the house after bedtime to work on this book.
Cindy Orr, for being a mentor and friend and introducing me to the wonderful world of readers' advisory.
Upper Arlington Public Library and Columbus Metropolitan Library. Go Buckeyes!

Craig A. Clark

I would like to thank:

Kathy, for your unwavering support and encouragement throughout my library career and beyond. And for your thoughtful help on this book.
Joey and Linnea, for indulging me in my sports obsession through you on the field and in front of the TV at home.
Cleveland Public Library, for your unsurpassed collections and fantastic staff.

Richard T. Fox

We would like to thank Libraries Unlimited editor Barbara Ittner and series editor Barry Trott for their advice, encouragement, and guidance. Finally, thank you Kate Mediatore Stover for offering up your initial idea for this book so we could knock it out of the park.

Introduction

As children we play games, some organized and some of our own making. We get older and some of us continue to play organized sports, others begin to watch and grow fond of favorite teams both amateur and professional. A few may go on to play professionally, coach or write about sports as an occupation, but the majority of us are fans and we like to read about, watch, and play sports. Finding stories is easy enough, as long as you are looking for a particular sport. Both libraries and bookstores organize books sport-by-sport, general to specific. This book aims to bring together stories of athletes, coaches, fans, writers, and the places that make sports loved across the world. We have tried to organize our book into categories that include multiple sports, varied athletes, and sometimes fiction and nonfiction together.

During our research, a few things became apparent: Runners like to write, and there are a lot of books on baseball, really lots of books on baseball, from histories of the game to histories of the teams, from players' perspectives to managers' perspectives, from fans' viewpoints to the beat writers' opinions. We can read about Negro and women's leagues. We can lose ourselves in the statistics of the game, from Hall of Famers to those who only pitched to one batter or came up to bat just once. There are hundreds of books of fiction on baseball. Great established writers and neophyte authors have taken a swing at that great baseball novel. Why is this? What is it about this particular game that has aroused the imaginations of so many? Is it because there is no clock to tell us when the game is over? Is it the superstitions that seem embedded in the game, hardly changing over its long history? The end result is that we have included lots of baseball books in this book. We could have written *Read On . . . Baseball*, but of course that would defeat the purpose of this series. In fact, there are some great baseball bibliographies in print. *501 Baseball Books Fans Must Read Before They Die* by Ron Kaplan (2013) and *The Baseball Novel: A History and Annotated Bibliography of Adult Fiction* by Noel Schraufnagel (2008) belong in any serious baseball buffs collection.

Another challenge of putting together categories is some of the greatest living athletes of this generation have not had recent books written about them. Michael Jordan and Wayne Gretzky are two good examples. Both had various books published by or about them in the 1990s, but today while their careers have stayed in sports, the later chapters of their lives have yet to be written.

Also, we did not find many books that were applicable to our lists covering gymnastics, figure skating, or other popular winter sports. These athletes compete at a young age and their memoirs are mainly marketed briefly after an Olympic season. Some athletes use their Olympic fame to write books as adults, but often the focus is away from the sporting aspects of their lives.

In addition, the stories in today's sports pages are the books of tomorrow. We will just have to wait for a while for those books to be written. Similarly, superstars like LeBron James and Derek Jeter have had some titles written about them, but it's not too hard to find them on the shelves, and the merit of the titles don't quite fit the scope of our book. Lastly, we stayed away from regionalism unless the book had broad appeal. Red Sox fans like Red Sox books, us Cleveland fans not so much. We could fill a whole book with New York teams, writers, and players, but we gave them ample space within our categories.

Enjoy our selection of categories and titles that represent some of the greatest personalities, stories, and writers in sport. Whether you follow a list based on one of our categories, scan the appeal factor that most interests you, or simply find a book and visit your local library to pick it up, then you have made two sports fans and librarians very happy.

Sports Defined

We have tried to give a wide definition to the term sport. ESPN has televised Scrabble tournaments, chess matches, and spelling bees. If it is good enough for them, it's good enough for us. For the most part, our categories contain stories about mainstream sports, professional and amateur athletes and coaches, and the writers who capture the tragedy and triumph of the games we play.

Criteria for Selection

- Books with positive or exceptional reviews
- Appeal to mainstream audiences
- Published between 2000 and 2013 or classic titles still in print

How to Use This Book

As we stated in the introduction, there are a variety of book lists organized by sport and genre in databases, library websites, and fan sites. Each of our lists contains well-reviewed titles relating to a theme across sports. Obviously, if one of the category titles piques your interest, please use the titles chosen to start on your reading journey. Each list has one book marked as a good place to start. Since we attempted to include a variety of sports in each list, if you are a fan of a particular sport, you can jump from list to list to see which titles appeal to you. The index should provide some help with locating particular individuals or events that have books across categories. Tearing out a page and heading to your local library or bookstore is not recommended, because you will ultimately lose the page and you may not have noticed the titles on the back. Happy reading! An appendix contains a list of websites that we used to help define our lists and a few that contain great lists of sports books.

A Note for Librarians

We understand that some readers want to read about a single sport, so we have included a "title by sport" index in the back. We also hope that you will use the book to identify titles that you can use as starting points to enter your collection and direct readers to your browsing collection or subject catalog. Finally, many of the categories listed here are a valuable resource for unique library displays that allow you to showcase a greater variety within your collections.

Symbols

 Movie

 Award Winner
- **Casey Award—Best Baseball Book of the Year.** *Spitball Magazine* **1983 to present**
- **National Book Critics Circle Award. 1974 to present**
- **National Outdoor Sports Award for Literature. 1997 to present**
- **PEN/ESPN Award for Literary Sports Writing. 2010 to present**
- **William Hill Sports Book of the Year. British Award 1989 to present**

 Appeal to Young Adult Audiences

 Start Here

 Starred Review—*Booklist, Publishers Weekly, Kirkus, Library Journal, Amazon Best Book, New York Times Notable Book, Sports Illustrated Top 100,* etc.

Chapter One

Character

The men and women who play the games, coach the games, own the games, and report the games create an interconnected and ever-evolving athletic universe. Today, with a variety of media outlets and social networking applications, the lives of athletes and others in sports are more available, open to scrutiny, and immediate. But the depth and emotion of a thoughtful memoir or biography allow fans and readers to delve deeply into the lives of some fascinating people in sport.

We have tried to add a few surprises along the way. "Unique Individuals" explores some great athletes with uncommon talent, and "Writers Play the Game" reveals that many writers wanted to emulate the great George Plimpton, who tried his hand at many sports in order to more aptly write about them. So whether you want to explore the great coaches, root for the underdog, or find an outstanding memoir classic or current, please enjoy this selection of the people who encompass the games we love.

Best of the Best—Great Athletes/Great Writers

There will always be endless debates on the subject of the "Best of All Time," but these books represent some of the greatest athletes who have had *great books* written about them. You won't find LeBron James, Michael Jordan, or Derek Jeter here; their books have yet to be written, and the later years are most telling to becoming unforgettable in the world of sports.

Creamer, Robert

▶ *Babe: The Legend Comes to Life.* 1974. Simon and Schuster, ISBN 9780671217709. 443p.

Thank goodness for the monks at St. Mary's Industrial School for Boys who introduced George Herman Ruth Jr. to baseball. Namesake for a candy bar and a curse, this larger-than-life character is one of the most recognizable names in sports history. Creamer presents a total biography, pulling no punches and revealing the successes and struggles of a giant of baseball. ★

Dodson, James

Ben Hogan: An American Life. 2005. Doubleday, ISBN 9780385503129. 544p.

Before there was Tiger or The Golden Bear, before Arnie or Chi Chi, there was Ben. The only U.S. golfer to win the U.S. Open, British Open, and Masters in the same year (1953), Hogan was the major force in golf in the late 1940s and early 1950s. Dodson had access to Hogan's personal papers and presents an honest view of this complicated man and fierce competitor. ★

Dryden, Ken

The Game: A Thoughtful and Provocative Look at a Life in Hockey. 2005 (1983). Wiley, ISBN 9780470835845. 308p.

A goalie for the Montreal Canadiens from 1971 to 1979, Dryden was instrumental in six Stanley Cup titles. After his relatively short hockey career, he became an announcer, writer, and eventually a member of the Canadian Parliament. His memoir is considered one of the best hockey books (and sports books) ever written, and along with great hockey commentary, he offers reflections on life beyond hockey written with elegant style and emotion. The 2005 paperback edition contains an updated chapter. ★

Hauser, Thomas

Muhammad Ali: His Life and Times. 1992 (1991). Simon and Schuster, ISBN 9780671779719. 544p.

One of the greatest boxers, showman, and activists in the ring and out, Muhammad Ali won his first heavyweight title at age 22 over Sonny Liston. Hauser interviews over 200 friends, family, and professional acquaintances of Ali and deftly molds those stories into a lasting tribute to one of the most charismatic athletes of all time. Critics note that this book doesn't delve into the dark recesses of Ali's life, but it is a grand testament of a heavyweight champion who has transcended his sport to become an American icon. Note: In the MOOD category, there is a much different Ali writing with his daughter about his faith in *The Soul of a Butterfly: Reflections on Life's Journey*. ★

Hillenbrand, Lauren

Seabiscuit: An American Legend. 2001. Random House, ISBN 9780375502912. 399p.

A truly American underdog story on several levels, Seabiscuit was an undersized racehorse that captured the hearts of the world in the late 1930s, and along with his equally "broken" jockey Red Pollard, they became beloved across the nation. A national best seller, the movie of the same name was nominated for seven Academy Awards. ★

Hirsch, James S.
Willie Mays: The Life, the Legend. 2010. Scribner, ISBN 9781416547907. 640p.
 Few players possessed the skill, grace, and artistry of Willie Mays. Most baseball fans have seen his famous basket catch made in the 1954 World Series, but Mays was one of the few players in history that could do it all: hit, run, field, and throw. In this authorized biography, Hirsch had access to the 77-year-old Mays, whose life in baseball (1951–1973) reflected a changing time in baseball and social issues throughout the world. ★

Leavy, Jane
The Last Boy: Mickey Mantle and the End of America's Childhood. 2010. Harper, ISBN 9780060883522. 480p.
 Jane Leavy says that she believes in memory and not memorabilia, and this meticulously researched biography of an American baseball icon puts truth to the statement. One of the greatest players to wear the pinstripes, Mantle fought through injuries his whole career, and still holds the record for most World Series home runs. Leavy conducted over 500 interviews and does not gloss over the rough spots in Mickey's life. ★

Outstanding Athletes—Outstanding Autobiographies

Athletes are not normally thought of for their writing abilities. Sports are a visual endeavor, and player's lives are presented on television and at events in vivid sound and color. Fortunately, the authors below have both the gift of athleticism and the gift of delivering excellent descriptions of their lives in prose. This section embodies well-reviewed, emotional, and thoughtful memoirs by athletes and writers across the spectrum of sports.

Agassi, Andre
Open. 2009. Knopf, ISBN 9780307268198. 400p.
 Driven by his father to become a tennis champion, Agassi was a dominant and exciting player from the early 1990s until his retirement in 2006. While he was a "rock star" in tennis, Agassi writes passionately and honestly about his career and upbringing in tennis and his shift from tennis to a life of philanthropy and family. ★

Dickey, R. A. and Wayne Coffey
 ▶ *Wherever I Wind Up: My Quest for Truth, Authenticity, and the Perfect Knuckleball.* 2012. Blue Rider Press, ISBN 9780399158155. 352p.

An unremarkable conventional pitcher drafted in 1996 by the Texas Rangers, famed knuckleballer Dickey won the Cy Young Award in 2012 and has quite a tale to tell about the journey. Deeply personal and intimate, Dickey delivers an emotional story of the dark times in his life, his reliance on faith, and his successes on and off the field. ★

Guthrie, Janet

Janet Guthrie: A Life at Full Throttle. 2005. Sport Media Publishing, ISBN 9781894963312. 398p.

In 1977, Guthrie broke ground in becoming the first female driver to race in the Indy 500 and Daytona 500. She details her life from growing up in Florida, studying engineering, and very nearly becoming an astronaut. A true pioneer in racing, Guthrie faced relentless criticism as she competed in the male-dominated world of auto racing.

Hawk, Tony

Hawk: Occupation: Skateboarder. 2000. HarperEntertainment, ISBN 9780060198602. 304p.

A pioneer in professional skateboarding, Hawk has his own video game and once had an amusement park ride named for him. He cheerfully describes his rambunctious youth and takes readers into his life traveling the globe, finding his way into adolescent troubles, and winning unmatched success in the X Games and other competitions. He retired from the sport shortly after this book was published.

Joyner-Kersee, Jackie and Sonja Steptoe

A Kind of Grace: The Autobiography of the World's Greatest Female Athlete. 1997. Grand Central Publishing, ISBN 9780446522489. 366p.

The subtitle is not a boast, *Sports Illustrated* proclaimed Joyner-Kersee the top female athlete of the 20th century. She is best known for winning six medals over four Olympic Games from 1984 to 1996 in the Heptathlon and long jump. She was also a standout basketball player for UCLA. This book offers an intimate look at the determination and success of one of the greatest athletes, man or woman, in our time.

Leonard, Sugar Ray and Michael Arkush

The Big Fight: My Life In and Out of the Ring. 2011. Viking, ISBN 9780670022724. 320p.

Sugar Ray was one of the most beloved boxers in the 1970s and 1980s and his popularity remains high today. As a boxer, he won an Olympic gold medal and world titles in five different divisions. Leonard pulls no punches in this honest autobiography recounting his successes, his bouts with substance abuse and other personal problems, and his rebound and the inner peace he has finally attained.

Pele and Robert L. Fish
My Life and the Beautiful Game: The Autobiography of Soccer's Greatest Star.
2007. Skyhorse Publishing, ISBN 9781602391963. 416p.

Although Pele retired from soccer in 1977, players are still measured by
his remarkable play. The only player to be a part of three World Cup championship teams, Pele remains immensely popular internationally. Born Edson
Arantes do Nascimento, Pele begins his story in Brazil and reflects on his life
in soccer that continued into the United States with the New York Cosmos.
Pele's recounting of matches and goals is especially fun to read.

The Lives of Great Coaches

Coaches teach and motivate the athletes on their team, but some coaches
transcend their teams and affect the lives of generations of players, coaches, and
fans. Life stories go here. There are many paths to coaching greatness as evi-
denced by this diverse set of superb stories of some of the most successful team
leaders to coach the game. We offer another category in MOOD that includes
coaching wisdom and advice for beyond the field of play.

Auerbach, Red and John Feinstein
Let Me Tell You a Story: A Lifetime in the Game. 2004. Little, Brown and Company, ISBN 9780316738231. 368p.

A truly enjoyable reading experience, Feinstein recounts the colorful
coaching career one of the greats in basketball. For four years, he sat weekly
at a Washington, D.C. restaurant and listened to tales shared by Auerbach and
his friends about basketball, rivalries, friendship, and life. Auerbach won nine
NBA titles with the Celtics, which ranks second all-time behind Phil Jackson
and the most with one team.

Barra, Alan
The Last Coach: The Life of Paul "Bear Bryant". 2006 (2005). W. W. Norton
and Co., ISBN 9780393328974. 608p.

The fascinating life of one of America's best college football coaches is revealed in meticulous detail in this outstanding biography. Bryant is best known as
the head coach of Alabama, but as Barra weaves the story of Bryant from growing
up as one of 12 children in Arkansas, through civil rights and televised games,
readers will share in a story that is so much more than football. Roll Tide. ★

Gilbert, John
Herb Brooks: The Inside Story of a Hockey Mastermind. 2008. MVP Books,
ISBN 9780760332412. 320p.

The architect of "The Miracle on Ice," coach Brooks was also a successful
college coach at Minnesota. Not a bad hockey player in his own right, Brooks

played for the 1964 and 1968 U.S. Olympic team, and Gilbert begins his story with Brooks as a youth hockey player. Gilbert became friends with Brooks while writing for the Minnesota Tribune, and he aptly describes the life of a coach who played no favorites, cut no corners, and led a team to the most unlikely of victories.

Macht, Norman

Connie Mack: The Turbulent and Triumphant Years, 1915–1931. 2012. University of Nebraska Press, ISBN 9780803220393. 720p.

Fifty seasons with the Philadelphia Athletics, Mack is the longest tenured baseball manager in major league history. The second volume is an exhaustive biography (*Connie Mack and the Early Years of Baseball*, 2007). Cornelius McGillicuddy Sr. won five World Series and nine American League pennants, and he was respected for being intelligent, honest, and generous in all aspects of his life. ★

Maraniss, David

When Pride Still Mattered: A Life of Vince Lombardi. 1999. Simon and Schuster, ISBN 9780684844183. 544p.

Lombardi, perhaps the most known name throughout and beyond the world of NFL football, had a coaching career with the Green Bay Packers that resulted in five championships including wins in the first two Super Bowls. Maraniss painstakingly separates the man from the legend and sheds light on the motivations and life circumstances that created the man who may or may not have said "Winning isn't everything, it's the only thing." ★

Stringer, C. Vivian

Standing Tall: A Memoir of Tragedy and Triumph. 2008. Crown Archetype, ISBN 9780307406095. 304p.

The current head coach of the Rutgers women's basketball team, Stringer has amassed over 900 wins and ranks 4th all time among NCAA coaches. An amazing story of success, perseverance, and grace through adversity, this well-written and inspirational memoir transcends victories and losses on the court. Stringer believes it is not only her job to be a good basketball coach, but it is paramount that she assists her players in growing into confident and successful women ready to tackle life after basketball. ★

Summitt, Pat Head and Sally Jenkins

Sum It Up: A Thousand and Ninety-Eight Victories, a Couple of Irrelevant Losses, and a Life in Perspective. 2013. Crown Archetype, ISBN 9780385346870. 416p.

The first coach in history to reach 1,000 wins, Pat Summitt is the winningest coach in NCAA basketball, men's or women's. Diagnosed with early onset Alzheimer's in 2009, this book is a reflection on the life of a Tennessee farm girl who became one of the most successful coaches in any sport at any time.

Wooden, John and Jack Tobin

▶ *They Call Me Coach.* 2003 (1974). McGraw-Hill, ISBN 9780071424912. 272p.

Put simply, this is one of the best books written by and about one of the best coaches in the history of sports. Wooden won 10 NCAA basketball titles in 12 years including an unprecedented 7 in a row. His coaching style and teaching qualities transcend basketball and are used today as a foundation for leadership in the business world. In the forward, Bill Walton describes Wooden's two favorite teachers as Mother Theresa and Abraham Lincoln.

Owners—Titans of the Game

Fans often see owners of professional sports teams only from afar: through luxury suite windows, on television courtside, and occasionally on sidelines. George Steinbrenner best epitomizes the outspoken "titan"; he was an owner that unequivocally spoke for his club. We read about trade rumors, team relocation, charitable organizations, but rarely do we read about their lives. Rags to riches, family dynasties, beloved and reviled, these owners are some of the biggest in sport. Notably lacking are books about basketball and hockey owners. The legendary Lakers owner Jerry Buss passed away in February 2013 and a book about his life can't be too far away.

Burgos, Adrian

Cuban Star: How One Negro-League Owner Changed the Face of Baseball. 2011. Hill and Wang, ISBN 9780809094790. 336p.

Elected to the Baseball Hall of Fame in 2006, Alex Pompez was the owner of the Negro League championship New York Cubans until 1950 during the pre-Castro era. He worked as an attorney, associate of Dutch Schultz, and entrepreneur, and scouted in his later years bringing talented Latino players into Major League Baseball. From his early days as a Cuban émigré in Key West to fighting for Latino rights in Harlem, Pompez was an engaging and remarkable man that is also credited with bringing the first wave of Dominican baseball players to the United States in the 1960s.

Colangelo, Jerry

How You Play the Game: Lessons for Life from the Billion-Dollar Business of Sports. 1999. AMACOM, ISBN 9780814404881. 260p.

The one time owner of the Phoenix Suns, Arizona Diamondbacks, and other sports teams, Colangelo grew up in Chicago and came from modest roots. In fact, his first career was in tuxedo rentals and he didn't do well there. He was the first general manager of the Suns, and from there his career took off. Part personal history, part business advice book, and it may be a little dated, but Colangelo tells a fascinating story.

D'Antonio, Michael

Forever Blue: The True Story of Walter O'Malley, Baseball's Most Controversial Owner, and the Dodgers of Brooklyn and Los Angeles. 2009. Riverhead, ISBN 9781594488566. 368p.

Some people think O'Malley should rank with Benedict Arnold as one of the great traitors in America. Others feel that he made baseball a truly national pastime, and that his relocation of the Brooklyn Dodgers to Los Angeles was a visionary idea. From politics, to integration, to relocation, D'Antonio sheds light on a colorful and revolutionary baseball owner. ★

Davis, Jeff

Papa Bear: The Life and Legend of George Halas. 2004. McGraw-Hill, ISBN 9780071422062. 544p.

Interviews of over 60 friends, family, and former players create this wonderfully detailed account of one of the founders of modern football. Halas was a talented football player in his own right, and he became sole owner of the Bears in 1932. He created the T-formation offense that lead to the dominating "Monsters of the Midway." From Halas early life to long past his death, Davis presents a complete picture of a charter member of the Football Hall of Fame. ★

Dickson, Paul

Bill Veeck: Baseball's Greatest Maverick. 2012. Walker and Company, ISBN 9780802717788. 448p.

As owner of the Cleveland Indians, he signed the first black player to the American League (Larry Doby). He also signed Satchel Paige who, at 42 years old, is still the oldest rookie to play in the majors. The man who is credited with the idea to plant ivy on the walls of Wrigley Field, Veeck was an innovator, a gentleman, and he had a deep love for the game.

Madden, Bill

▶ *Steinbrenner: The Last Lion of Baseball.* 2010. Harper, ISBN 9780061690310. 480p.

Visionary, bully, micromanager, winner, genius—take your pick. George Steinbrenner has left a mark on baseball that will last forever. He had his hand in national politics, forever-affected baseball television contracts, and free agency; and at one point in his career, he was banned from managing the team. Madden, who has reported on the Yankees for over 30 years, presents the man in all his splendor, candor, and fault.

Rooney, Dan

My 75 Years with the Pittsburgh Steelers and the NFL. 2007. Da Capo Press, ISBN 9780306815690. 334p.

Officially taking over the reigns from his father in 1975, Rooney is one of the most successful owners in pro sports. The Steelers have won six Super Bowls under Rooney's tenure, and his roots have always been in Pittsburgh.

It includes interviews with players and coaches. Since the publication of this book, Rooney was named the U.S. ambassador to Ireland in 2009.

One of a Kind—Unique Individuals

Certain athletes excel at almost everything they do. Jim Thorpe was a football player and an Olympian; Babe Didrikson Zaharias was a golfer, an Olympian, and a basketball standout. Indomitable characters that amazed on the field and sometimes off the field as well. Most are household names but one or two may surprise you.

Buford, Kate
Native American Son: The Life and Sporting Legend of Jim Thorpe. 2010. Knopf, ISBN 9780375413247. 496p.

He was an athlete who excelled in basketball, football, and track and field and was unmatched in his time. He won the pentathlon and the decathlon in the 1912 Olympics, but had his medals stripped for taking money to play baseball. Buford's account is meticulously researched and she paints a colorful and detailed picture of this American icon.

Cherry, Robert
Wilt: Larger Than Life. 2004. Triumph Books, ISBN 9781572439153. 432p.

He scored 100 points in a single NBA game! In today's age of 24/7 sports and overhyped athletes, Wilt "The Stilt" would have captivated viewers as much as LeBron, Shaq, Jordan, or Kobe. Cherry interviews a host of people who knew Chamberlain and he provides an intimate portrait of this Philadelphia native.

Freeman, Mike
Jim Brown: The Fierce Life of an American Hero. 2006. William Morrow, ISBN 9780060776824. 304p.

He led the NFL in rushing for eight seasons and he is considered one of the greatest to ever play the game. Fiercely independent, Brown left football on his own terms after nine seasons. Freeman portrays Brown's life after football as an actor, activist, and advisor; but he also writes frankly about Brown's troubles along the way.

Meyers-Drysdale, Ann
You Let Some Girl Beat You: The Story of Ann Meyers Drysdale. 2012. Behler Publications, ISBN 9781933016788. 250p. Y A

Drysdale currently is the general manager for the WNBA's Phoenix Mercury, and she was the first female athlete to receive a full athletic scholarship to a Division I school (UCLA). She was also the first woman to get a contract with an NBA team. Fiercely competitive and supremely confident, she is a true pioneer of women's sports, and she continues to be an advocate of women's equality in athletics and college.

Montville, Leigh
The Big Bam: The Life and Times of Babe Ruth. 2007 (2006). Anchor Books, ISBN 9780767919715. 416p.

    The legend of Babe Ruth may not be so far from the truth, but Montville attempts to uncover the facts with access to scrapbooks and previously undisclosed documents. There was an abundance of Ruth books written in the 1970s when Hank Aaron broke Babe's home run record, and this volume, written at a time of scandal and steroids, reminds us of the amazing feats of The Bambino.

Tye, Larry 🏆
Satchel: The Life and Times of an American Legend. 2009. Random House, ISBN 9781400066513. 416p.

    Alabama-born Paige, a star in the Negro Leagues, was known for his exuberance and flamboyant style of play. When he signed with the Cleveland Indians in 1942, he became the oldest rookie in Major League Baseball. Paige is a history of baseball unto himself as he spent over 50 years in the game as a player or a coach. ★

Van Natta Jr., Don
▶ *Wonder Girl: The Magnificent Sporting Life of Babe Didrikson Zaharias.* 2011. Little Brown and Company, ISBN 9780316056991. 403p.

    Sometimes called the female Jim Thorpe and arguably considered the greatest female athlete of the 20th century, she won three medals in the 1932 Olympics, was a founder the LPGA, and was a tireless advocate for women's sports. Van Natta recounts Babe's struggles along with her unabashed pride of being a female athlete and woman in a time before it was commonplace.

Sport Families

    This category came about as I was looking at an article on the Sutter's of NHL fame. Six brothers, they all played in the NHL in the 1970s and 1980s. Unfortunately, there is not a recent book about them. It's funny how some families seem to raise champions and these titles offer a look into fathers, sons, sisters, and brothers as they write about their lives together as elite athletes. There are multiple titles about the Williams' sisters, the Hull's, and the Earnhardt's, so we selected the most recent or the title that spoke partly on family.

Clavin, Tom
▶ *The DiMaggio's: Three Brothers, Their Passion for Baseball, and Their Pursuit of the American Dream.* 2013. Ecco, ISBN 9780062183774. 336p.

All but the most ardent baseball fans may not know that Joe DiMaggio was not the only professional ball player in the family. Dominic, the youngest, was a seven-time MVP for the Boston Red Sox; and Vince was a two-time MVP for the Pirates. Beginning with their mother and father, Giuseppe and Rosalie, Clavin presents readers with an intimate and provocative tale of an immigrant family with some boys who could play baseball.

Earnhardt, Dale and Jade Gurss

Driver #8. 2002. Vision Books, ISBN 9780446612500. 384p.

Dale Earnhardt Sr. is arguably one of the greatest NASCAR drivers of all time, and his son Dale Jr. is well on his way to becoming one of the greats himself. Jr. tells an engrossing and humorous story of his first year on the Winston Cup Circuit, and he weaves personal stories of family and growing up racing into each race of the season. Tragically, the season ended with Dale Sr. dying in a crash at Daytona, and the book ends with Jr. at his father's funeral.

Gronkowski, Gordon

Growing Up Gronk: A Family's Story of Raising Champions. 2013. Houghton Mifflin Harcourt, ISBN 9780544126688. 224p.

If there were a case to be made that athletic success is tied to genetics, the Gronkowski's would be the poster family. Father Gordon writes an inside scoop on the care and feeding of champions. Three of the five Gronkowski boys play in the NFL, another played professional baseball, and the youngest is a rising college football player. This is a rousing, firsthand look at an exceptional sports family.

Hanson, Dave and Ross Bernstein

🎬 *Slap Shot Original: The Man, the Foil, and the Legend.* 2008. Triumph Books, ISBN 9781600781155. 256p.

Ok, so the Hanson brothers from the uproariously funny movie *Slap Shot* were fictional film characters, but we couldn't help including a story of one of the Hanson namesakes (Steve and Jeff Carlson played the other two) as he writes about making the film and his life in hockey. From struggling in the minors to hanging out with Paul Newman, Hanson delivers a funny and intimate look at the making of a classic sports movie, and tells tales of the people who made it happen.

Hull, Bob and Bob Verdi

The Golden Jet. 2010. Triumph Books, ISBN 9781600784057. 200p.

Bobby Hull, the superstar left wing for the Chicago Blackhawks, offers a glimpse into his hockey life in this beautifully illustrated book. Bobby's brother Dennis played eight seasons with the Blackhawks too, and Bobby's son was a fine NHL player as well. Stories and anecdotes mingle together to provide a wonderful portrait of an amazing hockey family. A companion DVD with interviews, highlights, and clips from the Blackhawk library are included.

Manning, Peyton, Archie Manning, and John Underwood
Manning. 2001 (2000). HarperEntertainment, ISBN 9780061020247. 384p.

With Eli and his brother Peyton being two of the NFL's premier quarterbacks, sometimes we forget that their father Archie was also an NFL signal-caller. At the time of this publication, Eli was a quarterback at Ole Miss College and Peyton was beginning his NFL career. Both Mannings offer insights on family and football, but Archie's comments on the state of professional football are both informative and entertaining.

Williams, Serena and Daniel Paisner
On the Line. 2009. Grand Central Publishing, ISBN 9780446553667. 272p.

Serena and Venus Williams have won 22 grand slam titles, Olympic gold medals in singles and doubles, and numerous tournament wins. They have numerous books ranging in topic from children's biographies to business advice. While this autobiography is from Serena, she speaks candidly about her special relationship with her sister.

Yer Out!—The Officials

Umpires, referees, and officials throughout the sports world rarely speak out during their careers. It's only when a call is controversial that they get noticed. Announcers, fans, and reporters don't comment on a well-officiated contest, but a blown call can stay in the news for weeks. These titles offer insight into world of the men that keep order in the games.

Fitzgerald, Mike and Patrick Morley
Third Man in the Ring: 33 of Boxing's Best Referees and Their Stories. 2013. Potomac Books, ISBN 9781612342248. 244p.

We don't often read or hear about referees' opinions outside of the ring, but these short interviews with some of the fight games best refs offer a unique perspective on boxing. From officiating contests in foreign nations to providing a close up perspective of famous fights, the thoughts of the men that stand between the boxers pack a solid punch.

Fraser, Kerry
The Final Call: Hockey Stories from a Legend in Stripes. 2010. Key Porter Books, Fenn Publishing, ISBN 9781551683539. 288p.

It is often said that athletes have "God-given talent" or they are born to play the game. The same might be said of Kerry Fraser, who at just 20 years old embarked on what would become a 37-year officiating career on the ice.

Garrett, Kyle and Patrick O'Neal
▶ *The Worst Call Ever: The Most Infamous Calls Ever Blown by Referees, Umpires, and Other Blind Officials*. 2008. Collins, ISBN 9780061251375. 238p.

Blown calls, conspiracies, and a bit of nostalgia combine to provide insights into some of the most notorious decisions across the sports world. Comprised of nearly 100 vignettes ranging from professional sports, collegiate athletics to the Olympics, this book sheds light and sometimes holds court on officials' calls through history.

McCarthy, Big John and Loretta Hunt

Let's Get It On: The Making of MMA and Its Ultimate Referee. 2011. Medallion Press, ISBN 9781605421414. 380p.

"Big" John McCarthy provides an insider's look at the history of mixed martial arts (MMA) from its inception. From his roots as a police officer through his 15-year stint as the sports premier referee, McCarthy is a major reason for the popularity and success of MMA today.

Motley, Bob and Byron Motley

Ruling over Monarchs, Giants, and Stars: True Tales of Breaking Barriers, Umpiring Baseball Legends, and Wild Adventures in the Negro Leagues. 2012. Sports Publishing, ISBN 9781613210598. 240p.

Motley is the only living umpire from the Negro Leagues and his story chronicles a time when umpires traveled on the team bus. More than a baseball story, this book presents a first-person account of history through the mask of the man behind the plate.

Rosen, Charlie

No Blood No Foul: A Novel. 2008. Seven Stories Press, ISBN 9781583228289. 280p.

Jason, a promising high school basketball star, enlists shortly after the Pearl Harbor attack and returns from the war missing two fingers. Unable to play basketball competitively, he becomes a high school referee. Rosen is a sports pundit who shares his love of basketball in this poignant story.

Skipper, John

Umpires: Classic Baseball Stories from the Men Who Made the Calls. 1997. McFarland and Co., ISBN 9780786403646. 180p.

Skipper researched and interviewed umpires for the 19 stories in this collection. Reflections on historic games and pivotal moments in baseball, he also includes box scores, a listing of umpires who played the game, and a roster of umpires from 1876 through 1997.

Weber, Bruce

As They See 'Em: A Fan's Travels in the Land of Umpires. 2009. Scribner, ISBN 9780743294133. 368p.

Weber, a *New York Times* reporter and avid baseball fan, delves into the society of major league umpires. He attends umpire training school and walks in the eccentric world of balls and strikes, funny hats, and unique voices. Interviews with umpires, players, and coaches provide the basis for a unique perspective. ★

These Women Rock

Female athletes seem to have a greater burden when it comes to memoir. Superior accomplishment is not the impetus for their stories. There is a need to inspire future generations of athletes to "live their dreams" and "excel at life." Many female superstars have not written their stories yet and we are lucky enough to be in a front row seat for the changing landscape of athletics. Below are some of the best women in sport, some retired and some very much still at the forefront of their sport. (Note to future authors: Write a book about Sheryl Swoopes and Annika Sorenstam for adult audiences—please.)

Leslie, Lisa
   Don't Let the Lipstick Fool You: The Making of a Champion. 2008. Dafina, ISBN 9780758227355. 320p.
   Leslie was the first woman to dunk in a professional basketball game and she won multiple Olympic gold medals during her career. Teased mercilessly as a youngster because of her daunting 6'5" height, Leslie certainly has had the last laugh. She had time to write this heartfelt memoir during her maternity leave from basketball in 2007.

May-Treanor, Misty
   Misty: Digging Deep in Volleyball and Life. 2010. Scribner, ISBN 9781439148549. 296p. [Y][A]
   Two years after the publication of this book, Misty along with teammate Kerri Walsh-Jennings won their third consecutive gold medal at the 2012 London Olympics. Misty chronicles her early life growing up with world-class athletes as parents and details her struggles and successes on the court, in the sand, and in life.

Patrick, Danica and Laura Morton
   Danica: Crossing the Line. 2007 (2006). Touchstone, ISBN 9780743298308. 240p.
   One of the most recognizable faces in racing, at the time of this printing she was "only" an Indy car driver. Today, she has transitioned from open-wheel cars into a successful NASCAR career. Published shortly after her rookie racing season, Danica provides an intimate glimpse into the life of a girl who began competing in Go-Kart racing at age 10 and the challenges to being a woman in the mostly man's world of racing.

Solo, Hope
   Solo: A Memoir of Hope. 2012. Harper, ISBN 9780062136747. 304p.
   Solo writes emotionally and candidly about her relationship with her father, her soccer teammates, and her personal life. Not one to pull punches, this two-time Olympic gold medal goalie attempts to explain her actions,

motivations, and shortcomings. From the soccer pitch to *Dancing with the Stars* to magazine modeling, Solo is one of the brightest stars of her generation.

Ware, Susan
▶ *Game, Set, Match: Billie Jean King and the Revolution in Women's Sports.* 2011. The University of North Carolina Press, ISBN 9780807834541. 296p.

Part biography and part social history, Ware examines the life and accomplishments of an iconic American athlete. Title IX was only a year old when King defeated Bobby Riggs in the Battle of the Sexes, and King was at the forefront of the women's sports revolution. Most of the women on this list owe a debt of gratitude to King and others of her generation for opening the doors to college athletics and being vocal proponents for equality in sports. ★

Wellington, Christine
A Life without Limits: A World Champion's Journey. 2013. Center Street, ISBN 9781455505586. 288p.

An Ironman Triathlon consists of a 2.4-mile swim, a 112-mile bicycle ride, and a marathon run. Wellington won the World Triathlon Championships an unprecedented four times in five years. A fierce advocate for international development, she has traveled the world as an elite athlete striving to bring the world together through sport.

Voices of Sport—Announcers

In the radio era, the smooth and fluid voices of sports announcers brought games to life in living rooms across America. Even when television took over, I remember my father muting the volume on the television so he could listen to the radio announcers. Television announcers added auditory passion to the visual effects of great sporting events. Al Michael's "Do You Believe in Miracles—Yes!" defined the 1980 U.S. hockey team, and Howard Cosell was unique among peers and athletes for his distinctive nasal voice and candid questions in interviews.

Cohn, Linda
Cohn-Head: A No Holds Barred Account of Breaking into the Boys Club. 2008. Lyons Press, ISBN 9781599211138. 256p.

This native New Yorker played goalie for her high school men's hockey team and continued playing for the women's team in college. A pioneer in female sports broadcasting, Cohn worked for several radio and television stations before becoming a fixture on ESPN. She details the gritty business of sports journalism, her struggles with the boy's club, and provides honest and humorous commentary on what it takes to be successful in television today.

Eisenstock, Alan

Sports Talk: A Fan's Journey to the Heart and Soul of Sports Talk Radio. 2007 (2001). Atria Books, ISBN 9781416573685. 272p.

Travel to any city and you can tune in to several local radio sports shows. Addictive in nature, the shows provide an outlet for fans to support, complain, argue, and debate their favorite teams. Eisenstock visits several cities and interviews these local icons of the airwaves to find out why these shows are so compelling.

Gold, Eli

From Peanuts to the Pressbox: Insider Sports Stories from a Life behind the Mic. 2009. Thomas Nelson, ISBN 9781401604363. 272p.

How does a guy go from being a hockey commentator to becoming the voice of the Alabama Crimson Tide football team and NASCAR? Gold offers his story in a whimsical and conversational style, full of stories about his work for a host of sports and teams. He did sell peanuts too. Another Brooklyn boy, Gold has become a fixture in both Alabama sports and NASCAR. As always . . . Roll Tide.

Greenberg, Mike

Why My Wife Thinks I'm an Idiot: The Life and Times of a Sportscaster Dad. 2007 (2006). Villard, ISBN 9780812974805. 240p.

Most husbands can relate to the title of this book, no matter the field. Greenberg is one half of the famous ESPN team of *Mike and Mike in the Morning*, and he writes an intensely funny account of his life inside and outside of sports. It's refreshing to read a memoir about a successful and entertaining individual who doesn't take himself too seriously and realizes how lucky he is to make a good living chatting about sports.

McKay, Jim

The Real McKay: My Wide World of Sports. 1998. Dutton, ISBN 9780525944188. 293p.

Before there was ESPN or cable television, there was Wide World of Sports. A weekly sports show that literally crossed the globe to report on everything from mainstream events to obscure sports like cliff diving, McKay was the main anchor of the show. Here he offers anecdotes of his life in broadcasting including an especially poignant chapter on his recounting of the Munich Olympics tragedy.

Ribowsky, Mark

▶ *Howard Cosell: The Man, the Myth, and the Transformation of American Sports.* 2011. W. W. Norton and Co., ISBN 9780393080179. 496p.

Howard Cosell was by no means perfect and Ribowsky reveals both his strengths and his shortcomings in this thorough biography. Described as a skinny kid from the Bronx, Cosell was educated as a lawyer before entering broadcasting. The man who gave us "The Bronx Is Burning" railed for civil rights and defined early television broadcasting; Cosell will forever be a giant in the field of television reporting. ESPN's Chris Berman pays homage to Cosell every time he says "He could go all the way."

Silvia, Tony
Fathers and Sons in Baseball Broadcasting: The Caray's, Brennaman's, Bucks, and Kalases. 2009. McFarland, ISBN 9780786438150. 214p.

Silvia interviews and shadows some of the great family legacies of sports broadcasting to create a conversational history of this special group of broadcasters past and present. (The Carays have four generations behind the mic.) He describes the physical action in the booth, asks biographical questions, and presents his narrative in a conversational style that is quite intimate. It includes appendices with biographies, speeches, and articles of his subjects.

Stone, Steve
Where's Harry?: Steve Stone Remembers 25 Years with Harry Caray. 1999. Taylor Trade Publishing, ISBN 9780878332335. 256p.

Harry Caray is probably the most recognizable press box commentator in the history of sports. From his signature glasses to his famous rendition of "Take Me Out to the Ball Game" during the seventh inning stretch, Caray's humor and wit endeared him to Chicago fans Sox and Cubs alike. Stone was Caray's color commentator for 15 years with the Cubs and his stories of Carey behind the microphone and away from the field are entertaining and enlightening.

Out of the Closet . . . and into the Spotlight

When quizzed whether any homosexual athletes would need to keep their sexuality a secret in football, Culliver (49ers cornerback) responded: "Yeah, come out 10 years later after that." Well, some athletes have chosen to voice the challenges of being a GLBT athlete. As this book is being written, Jason Collins became the first professional athlete to acknowledge publicly that he is gay. Collins plays center for the Boston Celtics and his story can be read in the May 6, 2013 issue of *Sport Illustrated*.

Bean, Billy and Chris Bull
Going the Other Way: Lessons from a Life In and Out of Major League Baseball. 2003. Marlowe and Company, ISBN 9781569244869. 280p.

Bean was "average" for a professional baseball player, but in his insightful memoir about a life in baseball and a baseball life in the closet, he recounts his life growing up, his marriage (and divorce), and his pain at losing a partner to AIDS and not being able to talk about it. Three years after his retirement, he announced that he was gay and in his book he appeals to MLB to walk the walk when it comes to equality and fairness.

Fisher, Marshall Jon 🏆

▶ *A Terrible Splendor: Three Extraordinary Men, a World Poised for War, and the Greatest Tennis Match Ever Played.* 2009. Crown, ISBN 9780307393944. 336p.

Detailing the Davis Cup Tennis championship match of 1937, Fisher meticulously delves into the lives of the men at the center of the match: Don Budge of the United States and Gottfried von Cramm of Germany. With the war looming, political implications were rampant. It's ironic that Hitler's star tennis player happened to be gay as was his coach, American Bill Tilden. Fisher deftly weaves tennis, history, romance, and intrigue into this exciting story.

Griffin, Pat

Strong Women, Deep Closets: Lesbians and Homophobia in Sport. 1998. Human Kinetics, ISBN 9780880117296. 264p.

Griffin is a pioneer of LGBT issues in sports. This book, though a bit dated, takes a look at stereotypes, institutional bias, and challenges that lesbian athletes face in society. She is a founding director of an education and advocacy program focused on addressing LGBT issues in K-12 school-based athletic and physical education programs called Changing the Game: The GLSEN Sports Project.

Kanyon, Chris and Ryan Clark

Wrestling Reality: The Life and Mind of Chris Kanyon Wrestling's Gay Superstar. 2011. ECW Press, ISBN 9781770410282. 336p.

Wrestling fans may remember him as Mortis, part of the Jersey Triad, or CCK, but his real name was Chris Klucsaritis. Kanyon fought with his sexuality throughout his wrestling career. Tragically, he committed suicide before this book was published. Coauthor Clark finishes the story of a man living in two extremely different worlds.

Simmons, Roy and Damon DiMarco

Out of Bounds: Coming out of Sexual Abuse, Addiction, and My Life of Lies in the NFL Closet. 2005. Carroll and Graf, ISBN 9780786716814. 256p.

This book is not for the faint of heart as Simmons speaks candidly and at times profanely about his life as a gay NFL player. Between his drug use and promiscuity, coming out on the Phil Donahue show, and testing positive for HIV, his journey to self-acceptance is a rough one and a cautionary tale at best.

Tewksbury, Mark

Inside Out: Straight Talk from a Gay Jock. 2006. Wiley, ISBN 9780470837351. 288p.

Tewksbury won the gold medal in the 100-m backstroke for Canada in 1992. Today, he works as a motivation speaker, television commentator, and he remains active in working for gay rights. A bit more humorous than some other titles in this category, Tewksbury provides some fun and touching moments in this thoughtful memoir.

Tuaolo, Esera

Alone in the Trenches: My Life as a Gay Man in the NFL. 2007. Sourcebooks, ISBN 9781402209239. 288p.

    Samoa-born Tuaolo played football for Oregon State before embarking on a nine-year career as a nose tackle in the NFL. After his retirement, he announced that he was gay, becoming one of only a handful of players to do so. Of particular note are his opinions on faith and homosexuality. Tuaolo presents a passionate and honest look into his life.

Warren, Patricia Neil

Lavender Locker Room: 3000 Years of Great Athletes Whose Sexual Orientation Was Different. 2005. Wildcat Press, ISBN 9781889135076. 345p.

    Going all the way back to Achilles and Patroclus, Warren examines the history of GLBT athletes through time. Gladiators, fencers, horse breeders, and icons such as Joan of Arc and Amelia Earhart join the ranks of more traditional sports as Warren explores history, societal implications, and biases of the GLBT athlete. Warren's 1974 novel *The Frontrunner* about a gay Olympic track star, is considered a classic.

Yo Rocky—Underdogs

    Rooting for the underdog has always been popular in sports. Determination and resolve propel these stories of characters striving to be the best under seemingly insurmountable odds. Sylvester Stallone's original screenplay had us cheering in the seats as Rocky Balboa battled Apollo Creed in *Rocky* (1976), and these authors reveal the lives of people (and horses) who never gave up in their quest to reach the elite levels of sport. We didn't add *Seabiscuit* here; we could add it to just about every category, but it is a great story that would fit well here too.

D'Antonio, Michael

Tin Cup Dreams: A Long Shot Makes It on the PGA Tour. 2001. Hyperion, ISBN 9780786886470. 320p.

    Esteban Toledo is no Tiger Woods as the first chapter states; in fact, he is a self-taught golfer who started out by being a caddie (and a boxer). D'Antonio begins his story as Toledo is trying to qualify for his tour card for the 10th time. Growing up poor in Mexico, Toledo enjoyed a bit of celebrity in his home country, but this story of a "grinder"—a golfer just trying to get by on the tour—reveals the trials and pressures of professional golf.

Gardner, Rulon and Bob Schaller

Never Stop Pushing: My Life from a Wyoming Farm to the Olympic Medals Stand. 2005. Da Capo Press, ISBN 9780786715930. 352p.

Alexander Karelin was considered the greatest Greco-Roman wrestler of all time. Rulon Gardner, a farm boy from Wyoming, tells his story of perseverance and triumph as he bested Karelin to win the 2000 gold medal at the Sydney Olympics. But that is only part of the story. Before the 2004 Olympics, Gardner suffered a serious injury unrelated to wrestling but still managed a medal in the games. Rulon's win over Karelin has been referred to as the "Miracle on the Mat."

Krantz, Les

Dark Horses and Underdogs: The Greatest Sports Upsets of All Time. 2005. Grand Central Publishing, ISBN 9780446577038. 240p.

Not all individual underdogs here, but we like the vibrant photographs and the DVD included with this handsome volume. Jim Lampley of HBO Sports narrates the documentary that includes clips of such wonderful moments like Greg Lemond's 1989 Tour de France win, Louis over Schmeling in 1936, and the Jets win over the Baltimore Colts in Super Bowl III. Fifty great achievements by both individuals and teams offer entertainment to those who prefer long odds to favorites.

Layden, Joe

▶ *The Last Great Fight: The Extraordinary Tale of Two Men and How One Fight Changed Their Lives Forever.* 2008 (2007). St. Martin's Griffin, ISBN 9780312353315. 320p.

I remember watching the fight between Buster Douglas and the seemingly unbeatable Mike Tyson. "Buster who?" Layden takes readers through the fight and interviews the boxers, trainers, announcers, and others to create a stunning and exciting portrayal of one of the greatest upsets in boxing history. Not only does Layden deftly recreate the atmosphere of the fight, but he also examines the widely different upbringing and circumstances of these two remarkable pugilists. ★

Letts, Elizabeth

The Eighty-Dollar Champion: Snowman, the Horse That Inspired a Nation. 2011. Ballantine books, ISBN 9780345521088. 352p.

Human underdogs face insurmountable odds to become champions through determination, training, willpower, and faith. When a man finds a horse scheduled for slaughter and transforms him into one of the greatest show jumpers of the 1950s, it leads to a grand story of inspiration and trust on several levels. Harry de Leyer, Dutch immigrant farmer, saw something in Snowman that was apparent to no one else, and Letts delivers a heartfelt tale of an unlikely team making good.

Sagebiel, Neil

The Longest Shot: Jack Fleck, Ben Hogan, and Pro Golf's Greatest Upset at the 1955 U.S. Open. 2012. Thomas Dunne Books, ISBN 9780312661847. 336p.

It would be unimaginable today that a golfer would be crowned a champion while golfers are on the course with a chance to win, but that's exactly what happened to Fleck at the 1955 U.S. Open. Sagebiel takes readers through Fleck's early days, offers tantalizing details of the tournament and players, and also describes society and culture in post–World War II America. ★

Schaap, Jeremy

Cinderella Man: James J. Braddock, Max Baer, and the Greatest Upset in Boxing History. 2006 (2005). Mariner Books, ISBN 9780618711901. 324p.

An apt title considering boxer James Braddock was on the welfare rolls trying to feed his family when he was offered a chance to fight heavyweight champion Max Baer in 1935. Schaap's detail of the fight itself shines along with the colorful characters of Baer, Braddock, and manager Joe Gould. Set against the austere backdrop of the Great Depression, this story of a washed-up, down on his luck Irish boxer is a great American tale.

"I'll Play the Game"—The Sporting Lives of Writers

George Plimpton pioneered the idea of "participatory" journalism with his forays into baseball, football, hockey, and boxing. These writers provide first-person accounts of the dedication and perseverance necessary to play at a high level. Their stories are often humorous as they find they cannot quite succeed, triumphant when they do succeed, and deeply personal as they discover things about themselves that they never knew.

Coyne, Tom

Paper Tiger: An Obsessed Golfer's Quest to Play with the Pros. Gotham, ISBN 9781592402090. 336p.

Following in the footsteps of Plimpton, this book chronicles the odyssey of a man with a 14 handicap as he tries his hand at the PGA's Qualifying School. Coyne, a writer and English professor, also wrote the novel *A Gentleman's Game*, which was made into a movie starring Gary Sinise.

Fatsis, Stephen

A Few Seconds of Panic: A Sportswriter Plays in the NFL. 2008. Penguin, ISBN 9781594201783. 352p.

The author of *Word Freak* gets in shape, straps on the pads, and takes a crack at football. Like George Plimpton, Fatsis goes all out risking injury to body and pride as he lives, eats, and practices with the Denver Broncos. From players to coaches to owners, Fatsis discovers some fascinating truths about pro football, and a little about himself. ★

Hart, Jon
Man versus Ball: One Ordinary Guy and His Extraordinary Sports Adventures. 2013. Potomac Books, ISBN 9781612344140. 184p.

A freelance writer, Hart tries his hand at a variety of sports and sports-related endeavors. Professional wrestler, semipro football player, caddie, and a successful stint as a roller basketball player are just some of the events in which he participates. A delightful little jaunt into the life of a man who just wants to play.

Heller, Peter ♛
Kook: What Surfing Taught Me about Love, Life, and the Perfect Wave. 2010. Free Press, ISBN 9780743294201. 336p.

Winner of the 2010 National Outdoor Book Award for literature, Heller has recently received critical praise for his first novel *The Dog Stars* (2012), a graceful, postapocalyptic story of loneliness, loss, and discovery. Talked into taking surfing lessons by a friend, Heller narrates his journey through the waves and his revelations on life along the way. ★

Plimpton, George
▶ *Paper Lion: Confessions of a Last-String Quarterback.* 2009 (1966). Lyons Press, ISBN 9781599218090. 368p.

Originally published in 1966 and widely acclaimed as one of the best sports stories ever written, Plimpton tries out to be a quarterback for the Detroit Lions. The 36-year-old rookie didn't make the team, but his insider look at the game of football was revelatory and entertaining during the time before modern day 24/7 sports coverage. ★

Ryan, Tom
Following Atticus: Forty-eight High Peaks, One Little Dog, and an Extraordinary Friendship. 2011. William Morrow, ISBN 9780061997112. 304p.

Tom Ryan is a surly reporter and Atticus M. Finch, a Miniature Schnauzer, is his dog. What starts out as the enjoyable experience of simply hiking in the New Hampshire Mountains turns into a great challenge of climbing all of New Hampshire's 4,000-foot peaks to raise money for cancer research. While Atticus may not have changed much, Tom undergoes a series of reflections on life and family as the two of them face the dangers and the beauty of the mountains together.

Sekules, Kate
A Boxer's Heart: A Woman Fighting. 2012 (2000). Overlook TP, ISBN 9781590208113. 256p.

Today she is the editor-in-chief of *Culture & Travel*, but when she stepped into the boxing life, Sekules was a travel writer for *Food & Wine* magazine. What starts out as an interesting hobby and hip way to get in shape turns into an examination of female professional boxers as Sekules steps into the ring in earnest. This edition is updated with a new afterword by the author.

Shapton, Leanne ♔

Swimming Studies. 2012. Blue Rider Press, ISBN 9780399158179. 336p.

While she never made it to the Olympics, Shapton competed in the Canadian Olympic trials in 1988 and 1992. An artist and graphic novelist, she includes beautiful watercolor prints alongside her spare but emotional prose revealing her life under the water. Winner of the 2012 National Book Critics Circle Award for Autobiography. ★

Snowden Picket, Lynn

Looking for a Fight: A Memoir. 2000. Dial Press, ISBN 9780385315845. 304p.

What starts out as a woman looking for an outlet for her frustration at her failing marriage turns into an emotional and intimate search for self-discovery. Picket, a freelance magazine journalist and book author, immerses herself in the world of Gleason's gym in Brooklyn and learns the fight game up close and personal.

You Are Not Supposed to Be Here—Breakthroughs

Read about the sacrifice, determination, and perseverance exhibited by athletes who just wanted to compete. Jackie Robinson has become a household name as the first African American in Major League Baseball; his story is here along with some other athletes who struggled, persevered, and succeeded in competing where they initially were not welcome.

Ackmann, Martha

Curveball: The Remarkable Story of Toni Stone the First Woman to Play Professional Baseball in the Negro Leagues. 2010. Chicago Review Press, ISBN 9781556527968. 288p.

She has been called the "female Jackie Robinson" and she played in the Negro Leagues from 1949 to 1954. A testament to her talent was her playing second base for the Indianapolis Clowns, a position held by Henry Aaron two years earlier. Born in Minnesota, Stone was not always welcome in the boy's club of baseball, but she relished proving herself over and over again. Ackmann provides a provocative story of a pioneer player in a changing time for baseball.

Donovan, Brian

▶ *Hard Driving: The Wendell Scott Story.* 2009 (2008). Steerforth, ISBN 9781586421601. 328p.

Pulitzer-winning journalist Donovan regales readers with the story of the first African American to win a Sprint Cup Series race. Wendell Scott just wanted to race, but he faced formidable obstacles on and off the track. He also accumulated fans and supporters, most notably Richard Petty, as he competed in nearly 500 races during his career as a groundbreaking stock car racer. ★

Eig, Jonathan

Opening Day: The Story of Jackie Robinson's First Season. 2007. Simon and Schuster, ISBN 9780743294607. 336p.

Eig narrows the focus of Robinson's story by zeroing in on his first year playing for the Brooklyn Dodgers in 1947. Meticulously researched, this book examines all aspects of Robinson's groundbreaking season from the attitudes of fellow players to the reports in the press and public sentiment. Eig also tries to separate myth from fact to offer an honest and insightful portrayal of an unlikely hero.

Gildea, William

The Longest Fight: In the Ring with Joe Gans, Boxing's First African American Champion. 2012. Farrar, Straus and Giroux, ISBN 9780374280970. 256p.

Lightweight boxing champion from 1902 to 1908, most people outside of boxing don't recall the name Joe Gans. Gildea researched old film and other documents to put together a dazzling portrait of Gans, the societal pressures of the time, and the world of boxing for a black man in a time of overt racism. The story revolves around the title fight between Gans and Oscar "Battling" Nelson, a 42-round brawl in the Nevada desert.

Hnida, Katie

Still Kicking: My Journey as the First Woman to Play Division 1 College Football. 2006. Scribner, ISBN 9780743289771. 288p.

Katie Hnida was born into an athletic family where they picked lottery numbers by jerseys and had posters of athletes on the wall. In 2003, she became the first woman to score points in an NCAA Division I football game as a kicker for the University of New Mexico. Here she speaks candidly about the support of her family and friends, the troubles and harassment she endured in Colorado, and her ultimate triumph in college football.

Jenkins, Sally

The Real All-Americans. 2008 (2007). Anchor Reprint Edition, ISBN 9780767926249. 368p.

Here are three names most people recognize but may not realize they have a common thread: Jim Thorpe, Pop Warner, and Dwight D. Eisenhower. Pop Warner coached the Carlisle Indian School, a school designed to assimilate Native Americans into "American culture." Jim Thorpe was one of the players on this speedy and athletic team. Their opponent, West Point, had an equally daunting running back by the name of Eisenhower. A fascinating story of history, character, and politics in the early 20th century.

Muldowney, Shirley
Shirley Muldowney's Tales from the Track. 2005. Sports Publishing LLC, ISBN 9781582611075. 200p.

In 1965, she became the first woman to receive a license from the National Hot Rod Association and won three titles in the Top Fuel Dragster division during her career. Muldowney writes about growing up, falling in love with racing, and the hurdles involved with being a pioneer traversing the then men's world of racing.

Politicians and Celebrities

Some of our greatest politicians and movie stars were superb athletes before they entered public service. Some celebrities find solace or satisfaction in competition or simply participation in sport. Here is a collection of names you might recognize whose lives have intersected with athletics.

McPhee, John
A Sense of Where You Are: Bill Bradley at Princeton. 1999 (1965). Farrar, Straus and Giroux, ISBN 9780374526894. 240p.

Bill Bradley was an outstanding college basketball player, a Rhodes scholar, and a three-term senator representing New Jersey. This classic of literary nonfiction takes readers into the life of a college star, following him throughout his college basketball career, and offers a glimpse into why Bradley was so successful in sports, academics, and politics. McPhee's writing is superb and he has had a celebrated career in writing. He also attended Princeton but not at the same time as Bradley. ★

Moon, Vicky
The Private Passion of Jackie Kennedy Onassis: Portrait of a Rider. 2005. Harper Design, ISBN 9780060524111. 214p.

Lovers of horses and lovers of Jackie Onassis, when added together, most likely make up a large segment of the American population. Moon guides readers through a little-known thread in the First Ladies history: an intimate look at her life as an equestrian. Beautiful photographs accompany the short chapters that provide a history of her riding and competing, and reveal how she turned to her horses for comfort and solace during difficult times.

Schwarzenegger, Arnold
Total Recall: My Unbelievably True Life Story. 2012. Simon & Schuster, ISBN 9781451662436. 646p.

It's hard to believe that it has been over 45 years since Schwarzenegger won the Mr. Universe title at just 20 years old. His resume is too long to list but most know him as either the action star of film or, until recently, as California's governor. He burst onto the bodybuilding scene and enjoyed unprecedented celebrity and success that led to his movie career. Arnold aims to set the record straight about both his life's accomplishments and failures. Look back on his classic book too: *Arnold: The Education of a Bodybuilder*, 1977.

Stone, Matt and Preston Lerner 🏆
Winning: The Racing Life of Paul Newman. 2009. Motorbooks, ISBN 9780760337066. 176p.

Paul Newman is well known to the public as an iconic movie actor, but he was also a race enthusiast who co-owned a CART Racing team (open wheel), and successful driver in his own right. The authors interview drivers, engineers, and other celebrities to offer a glimpse into another side of the actor who won an Academy Award for his role in *The Color of Money*. Photographs of his cars accompany the story. It's no coincidence that Newman fell in love with racing after filming the racing movie *Winning* in 1969. ★

Watterson, John Sayle
▶ *The Games President's Play: Sports and the Presidency.* 2009 (2006). The Johns Hopkins University Press, ISBN 9780801892585. 416p.

Watterson researches sports and presidents to see how their sporting lives compare to the way they approached politics. Teddy Roosevelt receives top billing as the founding father of sports presidents for his involvement with reforming football, scaling cliffs, and wrestling. Many presidents competed in athletics in high school or college, and many had athletic hobbies like golf or running. Watterson goes deeper than a simple description of activities; he delves into questions about political decisions, political acumen, and the ethics of presidents; and he offers some interesting conclusions based on his research.

Williams, Esther
The Million Dollar Mermaid: An Autobiography. 2000. Mariner Books, ISBN 9780156011358. 416p.

The star of many Hollywood aqua-musicals was a one-time Olympic hopeful, but World War II interrupted her swimming career. She won AAU championships in swimming and later in life she was a commentator for Olympic synchronized swimming. She offers a frank and sometimes unpleasant examination of her life from growing up during the depression to her success in swimming and film (she was in 33 films), and she pulls no punches in revealing the details of her rather startling personal and professional life.

Winkler, Henry
I've Never Met an Idiot on the River: Reflections on Fishing, Family, and Photography. 2013. Insight Editions, ISBN 9781608870967. 144p.

Fishermen and fans of Winkler's film and television work will enjoy this light-hearted collection of anecdotes, family stories, and ruminations about life. Centered on his love for fly-fishing and his family's annual fishing trip to Montana, Winkler's quirky habits on the trip are revealed by his wife Stacey (he takes pictures of every fish he catches). An entertaining and humorous account of the wonders of family and fishing by a native New Yorker whose idea of a hike used to be a walk to the subway.

Chapter Two

Story

Most often we associate the appeal of story to fiction and its vast array of genres. From romance to mystery, the story is what draws in the reader. Yet, sport also lends itself easily to stories. A conversation about sports often begins with a story, maybe a tennis match played or a hockey game attended. In the retelling, it might become something slightly different or exaggerated. It might become fiction.

Like all smartly written nonfiction, sports books can transport us beyond ourselves and our known world to places and time and events we may not be familiar with. Sports stories can transcend the game itself. To the nonsports enthusiast, the appeal can be acts of courage, inspiration, or even love. We can learn from their exploits and experiences. Sports can encompass so much more than the event. The stories are those of endurance, competition, cheating, and seemingly unbreakable records. In addition to the athlete or game, there are tales of fans, coaches, writers, businesses, cities, and countries.

What follows is a somewhat offbeat collection of categories that try to grasp the breadth of stories contained in and around sports. Some look at the seedier side, others at the lighter side. We hope that most, if not all, are compelling in a way that captures what it is we all love about a good story.

Did You See That Game?

Greatest games or fantastic finishes. This list will highlight books that feature some of the most memorable or remarkable contests ever, or those "where were you . . ." moments that had to be seen to be believed. Several of those recounted here are long forgotten or remembered by only those who had a rooting interest. Others have become so part of popular culture that almost everyone will recognize their importance.

Anderson, Lars
Carlisle vs. Army: Jim Thorpe, Dwight Eisenhower, Pop Warner, and the Forgotten Story of Football's Greatest Battle. 2007. Random House, ISBN 9781400066001. 349p.

It was 1912 when these future legends met on a football field for what many consider one of the greatest games ever played: Thorpe fresh off his Olympic triumphs in Stockholm, iconic college football coach Warner, and Eisenhower, linebacker and future president of the United States. No one believed the Indian school Carlisle had a chance, but Warner and Thorpe had other ideas. *Sports Illustrated*'s Anderson does a fine job chronicling the game and providing the backstory for the three powerful forces. ★

Bechtel, Mark
He Crashed Me so I Crashed Him Back: The True Story of the Year the King, Jaws, Earnhardt, and the Rest of NASCAR's Feudin', Fightin' Good Ol' Boys Put Stock Car Racing on the Map. 2010. Little, Brown and Company, ISBN 9780316034029. 320p.

The 1979 Daytona 500 was a turning point for NASCAR's popularity as the televised race was widely watched on a little cable network called ESPN. Bechtel recounts that great race and the season that followed, which featured some of the all-time greats in racing including Dale Earnhardt Sr., Richard Petty, and Bobby Allison among others. Viewers had never witnessed such original characters and exciting racing before, and the stories of the drivers intertwined with social and political history make this a title not to be missed. ★

Coffey, Wayne and Jim Craig
▶ *The Boys of Winter: The Untold Story of a Coach, a Dream and the 1980 U.S. Olympic Hockey Team.* 2005. Crown Publishers, ISBN 9781400047666. 273p.

A "where were you when" moment in Olympic and sports history. "Do you believe in miracles?" was sportscaster Al Michaels's call as the clock wound down in the gold medal hockey game played in Lake Placid, New York, in 1980. Coffey offers a unique perspective on this watershed sports event when the U.S. amateurs took on a Russian hockey powerhouse. Driven by coach Herb Brooks who turned the players into a close-knit family, they captured the American imagination like few teams before or since. ★

Fitzgerald, Matt
Iron War: Dave Scott, Mark Allen and the Greatest Race Ever Run. 2011. Velo Press, ISBN 9781934030776. 336p.

Was this race between Dave Scott and Mark Allen the "greatest race ever run"? Certainly, when we consider the world of the triathlete where human endurance is tested to its very limits. Consisting of swimming, biking, and finally a marathon run, the triathlon is a competition that very few attempt. What made this particular race so memorable was how close it was throughout. Fitzgerald chronicles the lives of both runners and we learn in excruciating detail what it takes to be the best in this most demanding sport.

Frost, Mark
The Greatest Game Ever Played: Harry Vardon, Francis Ouimet, and the Birth of Modern Golf. 2002. Hyperion, ISBN 9780786869206. 496p.

Did anybody watch the 2013 U.S. Open held at Merion golf course outside of Philadelphia? As I was watching, I noticed that an amateur by the name of Michael Kim did a pretty good job over the weekend and finished in a tie for 17th place. That got me wondering if an amateur had ever won the U.S. Open? And then I sat down to write the annotation for this book and saw that in fact Francis Ouimet was the first amateur to do just that. And then I read that he did this by beating Harry Vardon, the most famous golfer of his time. The book does a splendid job of describing the tournament and one of the great underdog stories in all of sports. ★

Mailer, Norman
The Fight. 1977 (1975). Vintage, ISBN 9780375700385. 240p.

The "Rumble in the Jungle" held in Kinshasa, Zaire, and featuring challenger Muhammad Ali and champion George Foreman was one of the most anticipated sporting events of all time, and for once, the hype was worth it. Some believe the greater battle was of egos between Ali and Norman Mailer, but we'll leave that one for another time. Mailer recreates the event in all its drama while also giving significant attention to the political and cultural climate in Zaire. For those who were around for the fight, this will bring back a host of memories. ★

Reisler, Jim
The Best Game Ever: Pirates 10, Yankees 9: October 13, 1960. 2007. Carroll & Graf, ISBN 9780786719433. 280p.

There are many baseball games considered the "greatest ever": Fisk's homer for Boston against the Reds in 1975, Buckner's miscue against the Mets in 1986, and Carter's walk-off home run for the Blue Jays against the Phillies in 1993. But on this day at Forbes Field in Pittsburgh, in the seventh game of the World Series, no one could have written a more dramatic, thrilling script than the game itself. Adding to the drama was the Yankees having won the American League pennant 10 times in the previous 13 years and the Pirates having last won one in 1927. In this World Series, no fewer than 75 records were set. Mantle, Maris, Berra, Clemente, Mazeroski all participated. Reisler does a masterful job breaking down the game and profiling some of the key personnel. "What a game!" ★

Wertheim, L. Jon
Strokes of Genius: Federer, Nadal, and the Greatest Match Ever Played. 2009. Houghton Mifflin Harcourt, ISBN 9780547336947. 211p.

Wimbledon, July 6, 2008. Roger Federer, already a five-time champion on Centre Court vying to take his place amongst the greatest tennis players ever, was up against newcomer Rafael Nadal, just beginning to assert his court dominance. *Sports Illustrated* senior writer Wertheim chronicles the match in elegant detail and ably contrasts the two styles between the Swiss Federer and Spanish Nadal. A grueling, pressure-packed five-set match that ended in twilight, which no one who witnessed will ever forget. ★

Greatest Rivalries

Rivalries exist outside of championships. They bring their own drama and history every time the teams or players face each other. These books tell the stories of some of the most enduring and fierce of them.

Dyer, R.A.
The Hustler and the Champ: Willie Mosconi, Minnesota Fats and the Rivalry That Defined Pool. 2007. Lyons Press, ISBN 9781592288830. 309p.

One of the most watched sporting events of 1978 this billiard battle between the great Willie Mosconi and hustler Minnesota Fats became one of the sport's most defining moments. The competitors were the same age but couldn't have been more different in their personalities and style of play. Howard Cosell called the action for the television audience and Dyer's account takes us to the pool hall to relive the match. He also carries us through Mosconi's career as he ascended to become the greatest pool player of all time.

Eisenberg, John
▶ *The Great Match Race: When North Met South in America's First Sports Spectacle.* 2006. Houghton Mifflin Co., ISBN 9780618556120. 258p.

Believe it or not, way back when, the United States was obsessed with horse racing like we are now with football. Eisenberg's book takes us back to 1823 to one of the first sporting events to capture the imagination and attention of this youthful country. The race featured the top thoroughbred of the North against a fresh threat representing the South. While hard to fathom today, the two ran what amounted to a distance of nine Kentucky Derbies over the course of one day. ★

Fitzpatrick, Richard
El Classico: Barcelona vs. Real Madrid: Football's Greatest Rivalry. 2012. Bloomsbury, ISBN 9781408158791. 256p.

Fitzpatrick offers an absorbing history of these two Spanish cities' political and cultural flashpoints, and explains how this has matured into one of the fiercest rivalries in sport. Containing interviews with many of the key figures adds context to the story and will have you watching for the next time they meet.

Foley, Malcolm

Senna vs. Prost: The Story of the Most Deadly Rivalry in Formula One. 2010. Arrow, ISBN 9780099528098. 408p.

Foley's book takes us behind the scenes in the 1980s and 1990s through some of the closest, most bitter Formula One races ever run. Prost was a Frenchman and Senna hailed from Sao Paulo. They came from vastly different backgrounds and their personalities couldn't have been more unalike. Originally on the same F1 "team," their relationship deteriorated badly and they went their separate ways.

Taylor, John

The Rivalry: Bill Russell, Wilt Chamberlain and the Golden Age of Basketball. 2005. Random House, ISBN 9781400061143. 421p.

These two iconic superstars turned the NBA into the league it has become (for better or worse). Certainly, they popularized the sport beyond any reasonable expectations. Their matchups became legendary and intensely competitive. Their stories couldn't be more different and Taylor gives us the lowdown on how Wilt craved the spotlight while Russell was more able to sublimate his ego for the good of the team. ★

Tignor, Stephen

High Strung: Bjorn Borg, John McEnroe, and the Untold Story of Tennis's Fiercest Rivalry. 2011. Harper, ISBN 9780062009845. 238p.

Stoic Borg, flamboyant McEnroe, Grand Slam tennis. Need I say more? Some say the golden age of tennis came crashing down at the U.S. Open in 1981 when McEnroe bested Borg. The game has changed since then and maybe not for the better. The background lives of the players are just as compelling as the matches themselves.

Vaccaro, Mike

Emperors and Idiots: The Hundred Year Rivalry between the Yankees and Red Sox, from the Very Beginning to the End of the Curse. 2005. Doubleday, ISBN 9780385513548. 364p.

There have been many books written on the New York Yankees and Boston Red Sox and no one can deny the intense rivalry of the two seemingly perennial play-off contenders. While this book deftly chronicles the whole history of their rivalry, it is framed around the play-offs between the teams in 2003 and 2004. Both were thrilling series and Vaccaro does a fine job in the recounting.

Wilner, Barry and Kenn Rappoport

Gridiron Glory: The Story of the Army-Navy Football Rivalry. 2005. Taylor Trade Pub., ISBN 9781589792777. 224p.

This rivalry represents the oldest in the history of college football. It is made even more stirring as players are preparing to serve their country, and though the game is fierce, the real lives are just as compelling. Though struggling for national ranking, the service academies have done surprisingly well over the years, producing five Heisman Trophy winners and a number of national champions. This thoroughly engaging history of the rivalry entertains and enlightens.

Game Changers—Reinventing Sport

There are players, teams, and coaches that either individually or collectively changed the way their games are played. Larry Bird and Magic Johnson had a rivalry that caused people to flock to their televisions to watch NCAA basketball. Today March Madness is an entrenched American institution. Major League Soccer (MLS) was barely a footnote in U.S. sports until David Beckham appeared on the scene and caused attendance to surge. (The success of U.S. Olympic soccer helped too.) This category provides some examples of individuals and teams that have made a lasting impact on the game, some good and some maybe not so good.

Davis, Seth
When March Went Mad: The Game That Transformed Basketball. 2009. Times Books, ISBN 9780805088106. 323p.

Larry Bird and Earvin "Magic" Johnson. The year was 1979. The NCAA basketball season culminated in a championship featuring these two superstars. Davis's book takes us back to that season and to a title game that remains the highest rated basketball game in the history of television, a feat made more amazing by the fact that there was no ESPN and no cable television.

Dodson, James
▶ *American Triumvirate: Sam Snead, Byron Nelson, Ben Hogan and the Modern Age of Golf.* 2012. Alfred A. Knopf, ISBN 9780307272492. 378p.

Before the eras of Tiger or Arnie and the Golden Bear, three men captivated a nation and helped rescue a dying spectator sport during depression-era America. They drove their own cars to matches while trying to make a little money and entertain people. Dodson paints a detailed picture of the golfers, their competitions, and nicely sets the mood and history of the times.

Greenberg, Murray
Passing Game: Benny Friedman and the Transformation of Football. 2008. PublicAffairs. ISBN 9781586484774. 358p.

It's hard to believe that a young man from Glenville, Ohio, changed the face of professional football. Previous to Friedman, most football teams threw the ball only rarely and relied on a grind-it-out running style of play. Diminutive in size but strong of arm, Friedman forced defenses to change the way they played and thrilled audiences with his exciting passing game and running ability. Greenberg deftly recounts the life of a true pioneer in football. ★

McCallum, Jack

Dream Team: How Michael, Magic, Larry, Charles, and the Greatest Team of All Time Conquered the World and Changed the Game of Basketball Forever. 2012. Ballantine Books, ISBN 9780345520487. 352p.

Today's Olympic basketball teams are filled with NBA players from a host of nations. Not so before 1992. A *Sports Illustrated* staff columnist harkens back to the 1992 summer Olympics and the greatest basketball team ever assembled. Reflections by Michael Jordan, Charles Barkley, and Magic Johnson are remarkably candid, and McCallum's courtside seat and behind the scenes access at the Olympics adds absorbing detail to the story.

Miller, Marvin

A Whole Different Ball Game: The Inside Story of the Baseball Revolution. 2004. Carol Pub. Group, ISBN 9781566635998. 430p.

If one would like to truly understand the business of baseball and how and why the players' salaries have become so astronomical, Miller's book is the place to begin. When Miller became the first executive director of the Major League Players Association in 1966, owners who treated the players like cattle ran the game. When he left in 1982, the game had changed forever, maybe not all to the good, allowing for greater player movement and an escalation of salaries that continue today.

Sports Illustrated

The Great One: The Complete Wayne Gretzky Collection. 2012. FENN M&S, ISBN 9780771083617. 336p.

By the time Wayne Gretzky retired from hockey in 1999, he had set 61 NHL records. Today, most of the records still stand. The editors at *Sports Illustrated* have compiled the major articles about "The Great One" from his early days with the Edmonton Oilers to his rise as a team owner and ambassador of the game. It is doubtful that California would have three NHL franchises if, at least in part, it weren't for Gretzky, and his influence on this generation's players cannot be understated.

Wahl, Grant

The Beckham Experiment: How the World's Most Famous Athlete Tried to Conquer America. 2010 (2009). Three Rivers Press, ISBN 9780307408594. 320p.

Whether you watched MLS or not, odds are you heard about David Beckham signing a deal with the Los Angeles Galaxy in 2007. Wahl had full access to the world of David Beckham and provides a candid analysis of the outcome.

MLS attendance did surge during Beckham's tenure here, and MLS soccer never had so many fans or so much press.

Title IX—Leveling the Playing Field (Almost)

"Title IX is a law passed in 1972 that requires gender equity for boys and girls in every educational program that receives federal funding" (www.titleIX .info). Many people believe that athletics is the focus of the legislation, but it also applies to opportunities in higher education, math and science, standardized testing, and a host of other areas (www.titleix.info). While compiling titles for other categories, we noticed the theme of the effects of Title IX in several personal stories; so we have added them here along with a few general works on the topic.

Araton, Harvey
Alive and Kicking: When Soccer Moms Take the Field and Change Their Lives Forever. 2007 (2001). Simon and Schuster, ISBN 9781416575177. 256p.

An unlikely consequence of Title IX, a group of soccer moms formed their own soccer league in 1988 after missing out on sports during their youth. Araton's wife on being chosen for a team states, "no one's ever asked me to be on a team before." This is a story of camaraderie in sport as the women create a bond through soccer that helps them share life's problems and successes.

Blumenthal, Karen
Let Me Play: The Story of Title IX: The Law That Changed the Future of Girls in America. 2005. Atheneum Books for Young Readers, ISBN 9780689859571. 160p. [Y][A]

Blumenthal presents a highly readable and clear account of the history of the origins, struggles, and ultimate triumph for Title IX legislation. She delves into the history of women and sports, describes notable players in the development of the law, and includes personal stories from athletes, politicians, and others. Statistics and photographs round out the book and make it accessible for all ages. ★

Cohn, Linda
Cohn-Head: A No Holds Barred Account of Breaking into the Boys Club. 2008. Lyons Press, ISBN 9781599211138. 256p.

Native New Yorker Cohn played goalie for her high school men's hockey team and continued playing for the women's team in college. A pioneer in female sports broadcasting, she worked for several radio and television stations before becoming a fixture on ESPN. She also details the gritty business of sports journalism, her struggles with the boy's club, and provides honest and humorous commentary on what it takes to be successful in television today.

Hamm, Mia
Go for the Goal: A Champion's Guide to Winning in Soccer and Life. 2000 (1999). It Books, ISBN 9780060931599. 256p. [Y][A]

Hamm was born the year Title IX was passed into law and she is a stellar example of the positive benefits of the legislation. Among the personal stories of her childhood and life growing up with soccer, Hamm offers practical advice on the specifics of the game and the third part of the book provides tips on how to become a complete player both physically and mentally. A quote from Pele states that he is glad he didn't have to face Hamm on the soccer pitch; now that's an endorsement.

Joyner-Kersee, Jackie and Sonja Steptoe
A Kind of Grace: The Autobiography of the World's Greatest Female Athlete. 1997. Grand Central Publishing, ISBN 9780446522489. 366p.

The subtitle is not a boast, *Sports Illustrated* proclaimed Joyner-Kersee the top female athlete of the 20th century. She is best known for winning six medals over four Olympic games from 1984 to 1996 in the heptathlon and long jump. A standout basketball player for UCLA, Kersee is one of the greatest "first-generation" Title IX athletes. The book offers an intimate look at the determination and success of one of the greatest athletes, man or woman, in our time.

Sandoz, Joli and Joby Winans
▶ *Whatever It Takes: Women on Women's Sport.* 1999. Farrar, Straus, and Giroux, ISBN 9780374525972. 352p.

Focusing strictly on women, this volume will be of interest to anyone who follows women's sports or is interested in the development of the female athlete. The writers include the famous, including prize winners to the obscure. Many sports and topics are discussed including cycling, swimming, and Title IX. The book passionately reveals how sport has gained its rightful place in the lives of women and girls in society.

Strauss, Robert
Daddy's Little Goalie: A Father, His Daughters, and Sports. 2011. Andrews McMeel, ISBN 9781449402341. 160p.

In 1971 at the time of the implementation of Title IX, there were 294,000 girls playing high school sports. In 2011, the number was over 3 million. The explosion in participation has created a whole generation of father's supporting, nurturing, and training their daughters for athletic success. Strauss writes about the sporting life with his daughters Ella and Sylvia through a collection of anecdotes, some funny, some sad, but all emotionally charged by the love of a father.

Ware, Susan
Game, Set, Match: Billie Jean King and the Revolution in Women's Sports. 2011. The University of North Carolina Press, ISBN 9780807834541. 296p.

Part biography, part social history, Ware examines the life and accomplishments of one of the greatest female tennis players. Title IX was only a year old when King defeated Bobby Riggs in the Battle of the Sexes, and King was at the forefront of the women's sports revolution. Most of the women on this list owe a debt of gratitude to King and others of her generation for opening the doors to college athletics and being vocal proponents for equality in sports. ★

Fabulous Firsts and Unbreakable Records

Here are stories about athletes or teams that have accomplished things that once seemed unthinkable or records that over time have proven nearly unbreakable.

Barry, Dan ♔
Bottom of the 33rd: Hope, Redemption, and Baseball's Longest Game. 2011. Harper, ISBN 9780062014481. 272p.

On the night before Easter 1981, the Pawtucket Red Sox have a game against the Rochester Red Wings (Orioles). Although most of the players are forgettable, there are two future Hall of Famers there: Wade Boggs and Cal Ripken Jr. The game is tied after the ninth inning. So they continue to play, and play, and play. It continues into the morning hours of Easter Sunday. Why wasn't the game suspended? Who is in charge here? Barry relives the story of the players, managers, owners, and fans that attended this marathon game.

Bascomb, Neal
The Perfect Mile: Three Athletes, One Goal, and Less Than Four Minutes to Achieve It. 2005. Houghton Mifflin Co., ISBN 9780618391127. 322p.

In 1952, three runners were determined to break the elusive four-minute mile. Their journey made news around the world. Two of the runners, Roger Bannister of England and Australian John Landy, finally broke the record in 1954 setting up a showdown designated the "Mile of the Century" later that year. This race is the long climax to the book and Bascomb masterly draws the characters involved and recreates the event.

Echenoz, Jean and Linda Coverdale, translator.
Running: A Novel. 2009 (2008). New Press, ISBN 9781595584731. 128p.

Originally published in France to much acclaim, Echenoz provides a compelling fictional account of the great Olympic runner Emil Zatopek who is the only long-distance runner to win the 5,000 m, 10,000 m, and marathon in the same Olympics. It is a record that has stood since 1952. Echonez intertwines Zatopek's amazing feats against the backdrop of postwar communist Czechoslovakia.

Farley, Walter
 Man o' War. 1983 (1962). Random House, ISBN 9780394860152. 352p. [Y][A]
      Before Seabiscuit and Secretariat, there was Man o' War who won 20 of
 his 21 races, one of them by an unmatched 100 lengths. Farley uses the fictional stable boy Danny Ryan to tell the horse's incredible story. "Big Red," as
 he was affectionately known, set and broke turf records while carrying weights
 surpassing 130 pounds. Retired in 1920 after two years of racing, largely because no other horses would race against him, Man o' War had a successful
 stud career, siring War Admiral, the 1937 Triple Crown winner, and Hard Tack,
 sire of Seabiscuit.

Freeman, Mike
 Undefeated: Inside the 1972 Miami Dolphins Perfect Season. 2012. It Books,
 ISBN 9780062009821. 320p.
      The only NFL team to post a perfect season, the 1972 Miami Dolphins
 were still reeling from their Super Bowl loss in 1971 when the new season
 began. Hall of Fame coach Don Shula made sure they didn't forget how in-
 ferior they felt the previous year and reminded the team of that constantly.
 Freeman's book takes us through that epic season and is filled with detailed
 research and interviews with many of the participants. A feast for the football
 fanatic.

Kennedy, Kostya ♛
 ▶ *56: Joe DiMaggio and the Last Magic Number in Sports.* 2011. Sports Illustrated Books, ISBN 9781603201773. 367p.
      On a quiet afternoon at Yankee stadium in May 1941, Joe DiMaggio sin-
 gled to left field. Thus began a streak of 56 straight games where DiMaggio hit
 safely, a record some believe will never be broken. Kennedy recounts a great
 story that puts the 1941 season in historical and cultural context. Remarkably,
 1941 was the same season that Ted Williams hit .406, the last ballplayer to do
 so. Guess who won the Most Valuable Player award that year?

Montville, Leigh
 Ted Williams: The Biography of an American Hero. 2005 (2004). Anchor, ISBN
 9780767913201. 560p.
      Maybe the greatest hitter of all time, Ted Williams was the last baseball
 player to hit .400 (he finished batting .406) for an entire season. This biography
 covers his extraordinary life giving significant attention to 1941. There have
 been a few attempts at the elusive .400 since (George Brett .390 in 1980) but all
 have fallen short. Montville's book offers inside accounts of Williams's obses-
 sive development as a hitter and his constant struggle to perfect his swing. The
 last years of Williams's life were troubled in many ways and are also covered
 here. What remains beyond dispute are his unparalleled career including the
 magical 1941.

Mortimer, Gavin
The Great Swim. 2008. Walker & Co.: Distributed to the trade by Macmillan, ISBN 9780802715951. 325p.

> Mortimer takes us back to 1926 as four American women vie to become the first to swim the English Channel. He profiles each of the participants and follows up on their lives after the competition. What is often overlooked is what a media event this was at the time and that it became a defining event in the way women were perceived. Set in postwar pre-depression America, it is a grand account of a fabulous first and will appeal to swimmers, historians, and those interested in women's history. ★

Paper, Lew
Perfect: Don Larsen's Miraculous World Series Game and the Men Who Made It Happen. 2009. New American Library, ISBN 9780451228192. 421p.

> Game five of the 1956 World Series between the Brooklyn Dodgers and the New York Yankees is remembered because Don Larsen is the only player to have pitched a perfect game in the fall classic. This remarkable accomplishment by an otherwise ordinary pitcher is still considered one of the greatest individual feats in team sports history. Each chapter in Paper's book is a mini biography of the players involved in the game, including Jackie Robinson, Mickey Mantle, and Yogi Berra. Played at a time when baseball was still our national pastime, the book is a delight for any fan of the game.

Pomerantz, Gary M.
Wilt, 1962: The Night of 100 Points and the Dawn of a New Era. 2006. Crown Publishers, ISBN 9781400051601. 267p.

> Truly, one of sports greatest achievements happened on the night of March 2, 1962 when center Wilt Chamberlain scored 100 points for the Philadelphia Warriors. Played at a time when pro basketball took a backseat to the college game, his performance has remained unparalleled. Pomerantz not only provides an extensive narrative of the game itself, but also manages to deliver an engaging portrait of one of the great athletes in history. In addition, we get a sense of the social issues of the time, including the civil rights movement.

Endurance—Highest, Fastest, and Furthest

Sports can be so physically demanding that we watch in awe and wonder as superconditioned athletes compete. Mountain climbers, ultramarathoners, and kayakers are a special breed who needs an amazing amount of inner drive to compete at a high level. These books cast a spotlight on a few of the men and women who push the limits of human endurance and astonish us all.

Glickman, Joe
Fearless: One Woman, One Kayak, One Continent. 2011. FalconGuides, ISBN 9780762772872. 197p.

This book is a tribute to Freya Hoffmeister, the first woman to circumnavigate Australia alone in a sea kayak (at age 45 no less). Journalist Glickman follows Hoffmeister's 332-day voyage and creates a compelling page-turner that is hard to put down and even more difficult to believe. By the way, she did this faster than the only other person to have done it over 27 years earlier.

Jurek, Scott and Steve Friedman
Eat and Run: My Unlikely Journey to Ultramarathon Greatness. 2011. Houghton Mifflin Harcourt, ISBN 9780544002319. 260p.
　　Jurek has had a very unique career by combining ultramarathon running with a plant-based diet. He talks about his life and how he became a champion athlete while also recounting some of his most challenging races. The book includes recipes in addition to tips on running these most difficult of marathons. ★

Krakauer, Jon
▶ *Into Thin Air.* 1999 (1997). Villard, ISBN 9780613663618. 293p. 〔Y〕〔A〕
　　What is it about Mount Everest that so compels us to scale it? Could one write its history without attempting to climb it? Krakauer does both and his account is both riveting and terrifying as his quest becomes fraught with danger. Readers will wonder why some people must risk their lives and ignore their loved one's pleas in order to reach the summit.

McDougall, Christopher
Born to Run: A Hidden Tribe, Superathletes, and the Greatest Race the World Has Never Seen. 2009. Alfred A. Knopf, ISBN 9780307266309. 287p.
　　McDougall travels to the Copper Canyons in Mexico seeking to find the Tarahumara Indians who supposedly harbor the secrets of marathon running. The tribe is able to run long distances with hardly any discernible effort or injury. As an oft-injured runner himself, the author marvels at this ability. What he learns has as much to do with the way one looks at life as anything else. A *New York Times* best seller for over 16 weeks.

Paulsen, Gary
Winterdance: The Fine Madness of Running the Iditarod. 1995 (1994). Mariner Books, ISBN 9780156001458. 256p.
　　The Iditarod is the 1,150-mile winter sled-dog race between Anchorage and Nome. This is the story of author Paulsen and his quest to train for and run this unique race. His ignorance and fierce determination were probably both responsible for his eventual success. Told with humor and sometimes sadness, readers will be captivated by his unique story, though probably not enough to try it for themselves.

Sherman, Derek
Race across the Sky: A Novel. 2013. Plume, ISBN 978045229906. 373p.
　　Ultramarathons test the boundaries of human endurance, but they can be quite solitary endeavors. Sherman centers his debut novel on Caleb Oberest,

a runner who has immersed himself in the culture of running 100-mile races and has severed ties with family and friends in order to compete in these grueling races. However, when he finds himself in need of help from his geneticist brother in order to save the life of a child, they embark on a dangerous journey that could cost them more than they are ready to sacrifice.

Snyder, Amy
Hell on Two Wheels: An Astonishing Story of Suffering, Triumph, and the Most Extreme Endurance Race in the World. 2011. Triumph Books, ISBN 9781600785252. 251p.

Distance cycling is the focus of Snyder's book, in particular the Race Across America. Talk about endurance, both physical and mental, these athletes have it in spades. This is a behind the scenes look at the 2009 race. It will particularly appeal to those who attempted a cycling endurance race or just like to cycle long distances. The author interviews many of the participants both men and women, and their triumphs and struggles make a compelling read for anyone who likes a good story.

Williams, Geoff
C.C. Pyle's Amazing Foot Race: The True Story of the 1928 Coast-to-Coast Run across America. 2007. Rodale Books, ISBN 9781594863196. 322p.

A promotional stunt created by C.C. Pyle is the basis of Williams's book, which takes place on the eve of The Great Depression. A group of 199 men set off on foot from Los Angeles to New York City and more than 50 racers finished this grueling endurance test and the story is told in a breezy, entertaining style. While focusing on the runners, the race, and the promoter behind it, the book is also a nostalgic look at the roaring 1920s before it all fell apart.

There's a War On (U.S. Wars)

During the world's many wars sports have sometimes provided a welcome diversion and also served as a rallying point for a nation. This list takes us to some of the best books on the subject.

Algeo, Matthew
Last Team Standing: How the Steelers and the Eagles—"The Steagles"—Saved Pro Football during World War II. 2006. Da Capo Press, ISBN 9780306814723. 270p.

It is hard to believe today, but by 1943, the NFL was having a hard time fielding enough teams for a season due to World War II. A by-product of this shortage was the merging of two teams: the Pittsburgh Steelers and the Philadelphia Eagles. Algoe's book covers the story of "The Steagles" and how this ragtag collection of football players not only competed but also ended up with a winning record. The book also looks at the war at home and how life in the United States was changing in many ways.

Doig, Ivan
The Eleventh Man. 2009 (2008). Mariner Books, ISBN 9780547247632. 416p.

An old-fashioned storyteller in the best sense of the word, Doig's novel features 11 members of a Montana college football team that sign up to serve their country in World War II and find themselves separated and shipped around the world. When one of them (Ben Reinking) becomes a war reporter, he attempts to track down each of his former teammates. Unfortunately something odd seems to be happening: They are being killed one by one. Why is that? Ben's search leads him to learn as much about himself as others.

Fountain, Ben 🏆
Billy Lynn's Long Halftime Walk. 2012. Ecco, ISBN 9780060885595. 307p.

One of the most highly acclaimed novels of 2012 has very little to do with sports except that it takes place at a Dallas Cowboys football game on Thanksgiving day. Billy Lynn and his Bravo squad mates are there to be honored for a firefight that took place against Iraqi insurgents and this is part of a bizarre victory tour they are on. As the day wears on, Fountain manages to comment on many of the social and political issues of the time. Winner of the National Book Critics Circle Award for Fiction. ★

Hillenbrand, Laura
▶ *Unbroken.* 2010. Random House, ISBN 9781400064168. 473p.

Seabiscuit author Hillenbrand writes an epic biography of Louis Zamperini, a runner who competed in Hitler's Olympics and then became part of the U.S. Air Force during World War II. He was shot down over the ocean, left adrift for over a month, finally rescued by the Japanese, and became a POW. His story is remarkable and Hillenbrand does the story proud. She utilizes her many years of research into a gripping narrative that never falters. She not only interviewed Zamperini many times, but also family members, other POWs, and their families. One of 2010's most highly acclaimed books. ★

Lazarus, Adam
Super Bowl Monday: From the Persian Gulf to the Shores of West Florida: The New York Giants, the Buffalo Bills, and Super Bowl XXV. 2011. Taylor Trade Pub., ISBN 9781589796003. 235p.

Ten days before Super Bowl XXV, the United States authorized Desert Storm and thus began the Persian Gulf War. The book's title derives from the fact that with the time difference, the game was played on Monday morning in Saudi Arabia, Kuwait, and Iraq. A wonderful account of a great game that looks at sport as a diversion from the harsh realities of the real world.

Moore, Gary W. 🏆
Playing with the Enemy: A Baseball Prodigy, a World at War, and a Field of Broken Dreams. 2006. Penguin Books, ISBN 9780143113881. 306p.

A tribute to a father by a son about the father's remarkable life as a baseball player, serviceman, and civilian adjusting to life after World War II. This gripping story reminds us how many lives were interrupted by war and that those who lived couldn't always get back easily to the lives they led before the war. Winner of the Military Writers of America Book of the Year. ★

Roberts, Randy
A Team for America: The Army-Navy Game That Rallied a Nation. 2011. Houghton Mifflin Harcourt, ISBN 9780547511061. 268p.

For many years, the Army–Navy college football game has been one of America's most storied rivalries. One of its most memorable took place in 1944 at the height of World War II. The game provided a few hours of distraction for soldiers around the world. Roberts spent years interviewing those involved and his description takes us back to that historic time. Adding to the intrigue was the fact that Army was ranked #1 and Navy #2 at the time of the game. A terrific merging of sports and history.

Weintraub, Robert
The Victory Season: The End of World War II and the Birth of Baseball's Golden Age. 2013. Little, Brown and Company, ISBN 9780316205917. 464p.

The 1946 baseball season was special for many reasons. Ted Williams, Stan Musial, and Bob Feller came home from war. The country was ready to begin the long healing process and baseball would contribute greatly to that healing. Weintraub beautifully captures the season in all its detail and glory. ★

Political Underpinnings

When sports and politics intersect, athletes can inspire a nation and spur societal change. Unfortunately, when politics intrudes on sports, the results are not always positive.

Carlin, John
🎬 *Playing the Enemy: Nelson Mandela and the Game That Changed Everything.* 2009. Penguin Press, ISBN 9781594201745. 274p.

A quote from the book spoken by Nelson Mandela: "Sports has the power to change the world. . . . It is more powerful than government in breaking down racial barriers." Mandela was South Africa's president in the first free election in 1994 and decided that the best way to unite all the people in his country was through their rugby team, the Springboks. As they battled their way to the World Cup finals, that's exactly what happened. Carlin was able to interview most of the principals of this stirring story and undertook it with Mandela's blessing. The book works as well from a cultural and social perspective. ★

Mahler, Jonathan

Ladies and Gentlemen, the Bronx Is Burning: 1977, Baseball, Politics, and the Battle for the Soul of a City. 2006. Farrar, Straus and Giroux, ISBN 9780374175283. 356p.

Baseball is just part of the story in the New York City of 1977. Punk rock, the great blackout, and "Son of Sam" fought for headlines during that summer and some say the city was never the same. In the Bronx, the Yankees were fighting for a pennant and their battles both on the field and within the organization became legendary. Most of the conflicts were between owner George Steinbrenner and manager Billy Martin who was fired and rehired more times than we can count. Hall of Famer Reggie Jackson was also part of that dynamic team. Mahler does a fine job covering the events of that summer shifting easily from baseball to history to political battles, never failing to keep us interested. ★

Marannis, David

Rome 1960: The Summer Olympics That Changed the World. 2008. Simon & Schuster, ISBN 9781416534075. 478p.

The Rome Olympics starred among others Cassius Clay and Wilma Rudolph. They also featured the first doping scandal and were the first televised Summer Games. Marannis provides details of many of the most famous Olympians of the time while also setting the games within the social and historical context of the day. We agree that these Olympics were a milestone in world culture. ★

Margolick, David

Beyond Glory: Joe Louis vs. Max Schmeling, and a World on the Brink. 2005. A.A. Knopf, ISBN 9780375411922. 423p.

In 1938, Detroit's Joe Louis and Germany's Max Schmeling fought a rematch of a 1936 fight won by Schmeling. The rematch was no match as Louis won by TKO in the first round. Margolick focuses his book on the politics of boxing, and of America and Nazi Germany and the world on the brink of World War II. What makes the book equally compelling is the details of what Louis had to face in America and Schmeling in Germany, and what their lives were like in those countries after their boxing careers were over. He presents a good portion of the story through the words of the journalists of the day, which helps us clearly see the dominant themes of race in America and anti-Semitism in Germany. ★

Miller, John J.

The Big Scrum: How Teddy Roosevelt Saved Football. 2011. HarperCollins, ISBN 9780061744501. 258p.

For football buffs and fans of American history, Miller's book is a boon. A rare look at how American football was played in the late 19th century and how its early 20th-century transformation saved the game, with help from President Teddy Roosevelt. Early football was practically lawless, and as more and more players were actually killed, there was a public outcry to abolish the game. As a big fan, Roosevelt stepped in and insisted on a meeting with the coaches of the time and together they created the rules that ultimately saved the game and set it on its way to becoming what it is today.

Pinchevsky, Tal
Breakaway: From behind the Iron Curtain to the NHL: The Untold Story of Hockey's Great Escapes. 2012. John Wiley & Sons Canada, ISBN 9781118095003. 274p.

We've read the stories of scientists and military officials who defected from Eastern Bloc countries. This story is about hockey players who risked imprisonment, government retaliation against their families and friends, and the real possibility of being shot by border guards, all for seeking a life in America playing in the NHL. Pinchevsky has interviewed the stars that broke away as well as agents, general managers, and others who were instrumental in their defection. The book sometimes reads like an international spy thriller and is for fans of hockey and those interested in finding out how it turned into the global game it has become.

Zirin, Dave
▶ *Game Over: How Politics Has Turned the Sports World Upside Down.* 2013. New Press, ISBN 9781595588159. 225p.

A revealing collection of essays of how politics infiltrates and corrupts the sports we so love. Author Zirin's topics include racism, sexuality, and protest; and while many of these essays are quite frankly not pleasant for the sports enthusiast to consider, there are plenty of examples of players and teams taking a chance by standing up for what they believe is politically correct.

The Seedier Side of Sports

Are professional athletes like kids who never grow up because they are continually coddled and sometimes glorified? Are their antics magnified because they are in the spotlight? Here are fun books that give a glimpse of what goes on behind the games.

Achorn, Edward
The Summer of Beer and Whiskey: How Brewers, Barkeeps, Rowdies, Immigrants, and a Wild Pennant Fight Made Baseball America's Game. 2013. PublicAffairs, ISBN 9781610392600. 336p.

This is the story of the American Association Baseball League that functioned alongside the National League between 1882 and 1891, focusing on the summer of 1883 and the hard-fought pennant race between the St. Louis Browns and the Philadelphia Athletics. The stands were filled with fans who mercilessly heckled umpires and often drank and cheered relentlessly. They were able to do this because the Browns owner purchased the team for the express purpose of selling his beer. Achorn returns us back to a simpler time and not only gives us a good baseball yarn but a history lesson as well.

Bouton, Jim

▶ *Ball-Four.* 1990 (1970). Wiley, ISBN 9780020306658. 465p.

This is it dear readers, the first of its kind, the prototypical book that spawned hundreds of imitators. And few can stand the test of time like *Ball-Four*. Bouton's book, in diary form, covers a year in a baseball life, complete with adultery, hangovers, racial problems between teammates, and using uppers before a game. Told with humor and insight, the book was greeted with horror by the baseball community when first released in 1970. One of the seminal baseball books of all time. ★

Gent, Peter

▪ *North Dallas Forty.* 2003 (1973). Morrow, ISBN 9780688001834. 314p.

Still considered the greatest football novel ever written, Gent's classic was quite an eye-opener for its time as it sheds light on an NFL that while dramatically rising in popularity was still an anything-goes environment of drugs, sex, and violence. You know lots of fun and pain. Gent also touches on how the rise in violence in America itself mirrors that on the football field. He draws on his own pro football career to give the story its sense of authenticity. Made into a very popular movie that is ultimately quite tame compared to the book. ★

Lee, Bill

The Wrong Stuff. 2006 (1984). Viking Press, ISBN 978067076724. 242p.

This memoir by Bill "Spaceman" Lee was a best seller upon its release in 1984. He pitched for the Boston Red Sox in the 1970s and was part of the 1975 World Series team. Lee blends humor and personal memories into a quick, very readable tome. Teammates on this classic team included Luis Tiant, Carlton Fisk, and Carl Yastrzemski. And yes there are plenty of drugs and irreverent examples of Lee's lifestyle. You don't have to be part of "Red Sox Nation" to dig this book. It appeals to the nonconformist in us all.

Pearlman, Jeff

Boys Will Be Boys: The Glory Days and the Wild Nights of the Dallas Cowboys Dynasty. 2009. HarperCollins, ISBN 9780061256806. 406p.

The title of the book says it all. Troy Aikman, Deion Sanders, Emmitt Smith, Michael Irvin. This is the story of those Dallas Cowboys and how they went from perennial losers to winners in the NFL. Pearlman interviewed close to 150 members of the cowboy's organization for the book, and the anecdotes range from enlightening to extremely raunchy, but always entertaining.

Pollack, Neal

Jewball: A Novel. 2012. Thomas and Mercer, ISBN 9781612187235. 212p.

Pollack's novel is about the exploits of the South Philadelphia Hebrew Association, a Jewish basketball team on the eve of World War II. It's got enough sex, drugs, and violence for a Mario Puzo novel. Did I mention racism too? It has is a winning combination of drama, wit, and history too.

Richmond, Peter
Badasses: The Legend of Snake, Foo, Dr. Death, and John Madden's Oakland Raiders. 2010. Harper, ISBN 9780061834301. 358p.

    In *Badasses*, Peter Richmond chronicles the indiscretions of the legendary Oakland Raiders team of the 1970s with appropriate literary gusto. There was portly coach John Madden, Hall of Famers Fred Biletnikoff and Willie Brown, colorful quarterback Ken "The Snake" Stabler, punter Ray Guy, and "Hitman" Jack Tatum. Most of them liked to drink, party, and chase women, but most of all they loved playing the game and often winning. ★

Sanderson, Derek
Crossing the Line: The Outrageous Story of a Hockey Original. 2012. Triumph Books, ISBN 9781600786808. 388p.

    Former hockey star Sanderson is a perfect example of an athlete who rises to the top of his profession and almost just as quickly begins a downward spiral, losing much that he had gained along the way. Here he provides an explicit account of his hockey career and how his drinking problem eventually curtailed his professional life and what it took for him to get his life back on track. Gritty and honest, the book is a must for any hockey fan interested in its history and one of its greatest and most flamboyant players.

Inside Scoops—Tell-Alls

    These behind-the-scenes titles are diverting and intriguing, giving a more complete picture of the games. We may not always like what we read, but we can't close the book.

Auker, Elden and Tom Keegan
Sleeper Cars and Flannel Uniforms: A Lifetime of Memories from Striking Out the Babe to Teeing It Up with the President. 2001. Triumph Books, ISBN 9781572438248. 224p.

    Auker was a pitcher in the 1930s, and this is his memoir of life in the major leagues. He recalls pitching against Satchel Paige, Lou Gehrig, Hank Greenberg, and Ted Williams. While this book falls under our category of *Inside Scoops*, it is certainly not the tell-all that *Ball-Four* is, though there are plenty of shenanigans to go around. More of a gentle, honest account that seldom fails to endear. For all fans of baseball history.

Bissinger, Buzz
Three Nights in August: Strategy, Heartbreak, and Joy Inside the Mind of a Manager. 2005. Houghton Mifflin, ISBN 9780618405442. 280p.

Bissinger's book gives a very unique perspective on baseball through the prism of one three-game series in 2003 between the St. Louis Cardinals and the Chicago Cubs. Most of what we see is through the eyes of legendary manager Tony LaRussa of the Cardinals. Given complete access to LaRussa and the team, we gain insight into baseball technique and strategy that will be of interest to even the most learned baseball fan. A smooth and lively narrative that never gets bogged down in too much detail. ★

Cook, Kevin

The Last Headbangers: NFL Football in the Rowdy, Reckless 70's—the Era That Created Modern Sports. 2012. W. W. Norton, ISBN 9780393080162. 278p.

The NFL grew up in the 1970s, setting it well on its way to becoming the national obsession it is today. The book begins in the early 1970s when steroids were legal and Franco Harris hitchhiked to practice. In 10 years, the sport was on the road to becoming the multibillion dollar enterprise we know and love. Drawing on interviews with many iconic players of the time who reveal details of late-night carousing and other misadventures, we get the inside scoop on a transformative decade in the NFL.

Hayhurst, Dirk

▶ *The Bullpen Gospels: Major League Dreams of a Minor League Veteran.* 2010. Citadel Press, ISBN 9780806531434. 340p.

Hayhurst's book takes readers back to 2003 when he was a pitcher in the San Diego Padres minor league system. He moves up and down between different levels of minor league ball, and along the way, he recounts life in the bushes. Never sugarcoated and sometimes brutally honest, the author shares the drudgery and the hope that is the life of minor leaguers, some clearly destined to make it to the top and others only filler for their teams.

Jenkins, Dan

Dead Solid Perfect. 2000 (1974). Anchor, ISBN 9780385498852. 256p.

A hilarious novel set in the world of the PGA tour and considered a classic. Jenkins's language is often profane, but his humor is spot on. Besides golf, Jenkins pokes fun at love, Texas, and gambling. Mostly good-natured, this book is an enjoyable way to spend an afternoon away from those dreaded links.

McEnroe, Patrick

Hardcourt Confidential: Tales from Twenty Years in the Pro Tennis Trenches. 2010. Hyperion, ISBN 9781401323813. 305p.

Not to be confused with bad boy, short-tempered brother John, Patrick was a pretty good tennis player in his own right. He was a top 30 singles and top 3 doubles player and is a very successful analyst for ESPN. Patrick hung around the tour long enough to see plenty of dirt and offers an unfiltered look at it all. There is much here for the serious tennis fan as well as the casual observer. Your serve . . .

Reilly, Rick

Who's Your Caddy: Looping for the Great, Near Great, and Reprobates of Golf.
2003. Doubleday, ISBN 9780385488853. 261p.

   In this hilarious account of the world of pro golfing, *Sports Illustrated*
columnist Reilly carried bags for some very famous golfers, including Jack
Nicklaus and John Daly. At times, Reilly turns more serious recounting the
uphill battle faced by Casey Martin when he challenged the Supreme Court
ruling that he could not play with a cart, and the story of Bob Martin, one of
the top blind golfers in the world.

Williams, Jayson

*Loose Balls: Easy Money, Hard Fouls, Cheap Laughs, and True Love in the
NBA.* 2001. Doubleday, ISBN 9780767905695. 276p.

   Williams, former NBA player for Nets and 76ers, takes an irreverent look
at life in pro basketball, and provides the inside scoop on dozens of players,
coaches, refs, cheerleaders, and fans across the country. He also gives an account of his own life, including his wild early days to more recent charity work.
Williams describes growing up in a mixed-race family and the prejudices they
encountered in South Carolina. An honest account of the life of an NBA player.

Cheaters Never Win

   The difference between the great and also-ran in professional sports is
smaller than one might think. There is tremendous pressure to be the best in
professional sports. Dale Earnhardt may have said it best: "Second place is just
the first loser." That is why many athletes in a multitude of sports have used steroids to gain a competitive edge. And the thrill of competing sometimes is not
enough, so athletes look to satisfy their urge through gambling. Here are some
books that reveal how far they can fall when caught.

Asinof, Eliot

▶ *Eight Men Out: The Black Sox and the 1919 World Series.* 2000 (1963).
Holt, ISBN 9780805065374. 336p.

   This timeless classic is not a story of ballplayers cheating to win, but to lose.
The Chicago White Sox of 1919 were the undisputed top team in the game with
greats at almost every position. Buck Weaver, Eddie Cicotte, and Joe ("Say It
Ain't So") Jackson were just a few. Their owner, Charles Comiskey was famous
for not paying his ballplayers what they were worth. So when gamblers approached the players about "throwing" games in the World Series, they strongly
considered it. Engrossing, clear-headed, and nearly impossible to put down. ★

Donaghy, Tim

Personal Foul: A First-Person Account of the Scandal That Rocked the NBA.
2010. Four Daughters LLC, ISBN 9780615362632. 268p.

As a fan of professional sports, the last thing we want to know is that a game has been fixed. When we block out a few hours of our day with a favorite beverage and team, all we ask is for a fair shot at victory. Former NBA referee Donaghy's story is an eye-opener and a sobering reminder of what we as fans don't know about the games we love.

Frankie, Christopher

Nailed!: The Improbable Rise and Spectacular Fall of Lenny Dykstra. 2013. Running Press, ISBN 9780762447992. 288p.

Dykstra was a major league baseball player in the 1980s and 1990s for the Mets and Phillies. He played the game hard-nosed and people rooted for him. He was also a steroid user, hard drinker, and womanizer. After his playing days were over, he became a top stock forecaster and lived the high life until it all came crashing down amid charges of credit card fraud and grand theft. He ultimately pled guilty to three felonies in federal court and in 2012 was sentenced to over six years in prison.

Hamilton, Tyler and Daniel Coyle ♛

▶ *The Secret Race: Inside the Hidden World of the Tour de France: Doping, Cover-ups, and Winning at All Costs.* 2012. Bantam, ISBN 9780345530417. 304p.

Former Olympic gold medal cyclist Hamilton takes us behind the scenes of the cycling world to reveal the truths about doping and the great lengths to which athletes (including Lance Armstrong) go to keep their competitive edge. The book spares us no detail in its quest to reveal all that goes on in this most competitive of sports.

Moore, Richard

Dirtiest Race in History: Ben Johnson, Carl Lewis, and the Olympic 100m Final. 2012. Wisden, ISBN 9781408135952. 320p.

Moore looks back in detail at the intense rivalry and questions of drug use at the 1988 Seoul Olympics. Six of the eight finalists in the 100 m either tested positive for drugs or admitted using some form of drugs, including Carl Lewis. Although the gold medal was taken from Johnson and given to Lewis, Moore paints Johnson as the more sympathetic of the two. ★

Rose, Pete and Rick Hill

My Prison without Bars. 2004. Rodale Books, ISBN 9781579549275. 336p.

Written by Rose to make a case for his induction into the Baseball Hall of Fame, this book will appeal mainly to those who are intrigued by both his record breaking accomplishments and his almost unprecedented fall from grace. In the end, Rose finally admits that he bet on baseball games but denies ever betting on games his teams were involved in. The same obsessiveness and passion he had for baseball may have also contributed to his downfall. A subjective account of an embarrassing climax to a brilliant career.

Thompson, Teri et al.

American Icon: The Fall of Roger Clemens and the Rise of Steroids in America's Pastime. 2009. Knopf, ISBN 9780307271808. 454p.

> No story epitomizes the steroid era in baseball more than that of ace right-handed pitcher Clemens. A sure Hall of Famer who couldn't quit the game that defined him; his epic downfall is a tale of drugs, lies, and cheating. How did this all happen and who is responsible? Released in 2007, the *Mitchell Report* laid waste to all the awards and accolades that came Clemens's way. In its wake was a fallen hero. ★

Wolf, David

Foul! The Connie Hawkins Story. 1972. Warner, ISBN 9780446689700. 511p. [Y][A]

> Hawkins was the pretelevision era Michael Jordan or Julius Erving. His dunks were legendary, but by the time he got to the NBA, his best years were behind him. In college, Hawkins was accused of helping bettors "fix" games and in the heat of questioning by authorities, he confessed to things he didn't do. He was expelled from college and blacklisted by the NBA. A heartrending story that leaves one shaking their head at the injustice in the world; this is considered to be one of the greatest sports books of all time.

High School Hopes and Dreams

For many small towns, high school athletics play a major role within the community. Being the best is only one part of the story. The hopes and emotions of an entire region can get caught up in the success or failure of their local high school team. In *Friday Night Lights*, Buzz Bissinger's experience in moving his family to a small Texas town touched a chord in readers across America so much that it was eventually turned into a movie and television show. In many ways, all the books on this list have the power to do the same.

Atkinson, Jay

Ice Time: A Tale of Fathers, Sons, and Hometown Heroes. 2001. Crown Publishers, ISBN 9780609607060. 257p.

> Atkinson shines a light on his hometown and its ties to hockey when he returns home to be assistant coach of the Methuen, Massachusetts Rangers varsity hockey team, and shares his passion for the game with his son. As he details his life in hockey growing up in a small town, we realize he is not so much reliving his past glories as he is helping us to see the splendor in our own pasts.

Ballard, Chris

One Shot at Forever: A Small Town, an Unlikely Coach, and a Magical Baseball Season. 2012. Hyperion, ISBN 9781401324384. 254p.

> A small town high school baseball team, an inspirational coach, and an unlikely run for the state championship in Illinois, this book has cross appeal

for those looking for character, story, or setting. Throw in mood and language, too, because it evokes heartfelt emotions as Ballard tells the tale of the Macon Ironmen and their unlikely rise to the high school baseball state finals.

Bissinger, H. G.

▶ 🎬 *Friday Night Lights: A Town, a Team and a Dream.* 1990. Da Capo Press, ISBN 9780201196771. 357p. [Y][A]

In a city with nothing much to do, high school football is the rallying point for most of its populace. Bissinger moves his wife and children to Odessa, Texas, to experience firsthand what it was like to live in a small town that lives and dies with the winningest high school football team in Texas history, the Permian Panthers. A *New York Times* #1 best seller, this book captured the imagination of readers all over America. ★

Kreider, Mark

Four Days of Glory: Wrestling with the Soul of the American Heartland. 2007. HarperCollins, ISBN 9780060823184. 262p.

Wrestling and Iowa—the words go together like peanut butter and jelly. Kreider's story follows two high school wrestlers as they try to accomplish the rarest of feats: four-time state champions. This tale of drama, sacrifice, and commitment will have you rooting for them and shaking your head in dismay at the perceived importance of it all.

Mealer, Bryan

Muck City: Winning and Losing in Football's Forgotten Town. 2012. Crown Archetype, ISBN 9780307888624. 322p.

Appealing to fans of *Friday Night Lights*, this is another story of small-town America and its obsession with and redemption from high school football. Again, less about football and more about family and the struggle to escape from poverty, this is a stirring tale of sports as a means of dealing with a sordid daily life. ★

O'Brien, Keith

Outside Shot: Big Dreams, Hard Times, and One Counties Quest for Basketball Greatness. 2013. St. Martin's Press, ISBN 9781250000330. 309p.

Kentucky basketball is taken seriously at both the high school and college levels. The expectations are especially high for the Cardinals of Scott County High School. Championships were common once, but times changed; and the love affair between the fans and players began to wane. The book also focuses on race, economics, and self-identity. A fast-paced narrative will have you rooting for these kids to succeed.

Oppenheimer, Mark

Wisenheimer: A Childhood Subject to Debate. 2011. Free Press, ISBN 9781439128640. 241p. [Y][A]

As a child, Oppenheimer had a gift with words yet could find no useful application for it, often getting into trouble for being a "wisenheimer." In junior high school, he discovered the debate team and it changed his life. His journey is funny, touching, and relatable to the nerd in all of us.

Wilson, Steve
The Boys from Little Mexico: A Season Chasing the American Dream. 2009. Beacon Press, ISBN 9780807021675. 225p.

A high school soccer team in Oregon manages to field a strong team every year but falls just short of a title. The year in focus is 2005, and most of the players on the team are poor and Mexican. We get to know the players, coaches, and parents as they strive to battle their lack of belief in their ability to succeed.

Bubble Gum in Every Pack—Collectibles

It might start with a cheap pack of football or baseball cards, which used to include a yummy piece of bubble gum. Maybe you held onto some of those cards for decades or found them in a box in the attic years later. You may have stopped at your local library to see if they were worth anything. This list looks at sports memorabilia and collectibles.

Block, Lawrence
The Burglar Who Traded Ted Williams. 2005 (1994). HarperTorch, ISBN 9780060731441. 384p.

The first in a series of mysteries by the Edgar Award–winning Block featuring bookseller and former burglar Bernie Rhodenbarr. When his current landlord raises his rent, Rhodenbarr resorts to his former profession, and while stealing cash, comes across a dead body and gets wrongly accused of taking a valuable baseball card collection. He sets out to find the real thief and along the way, we encounter romance, eccentric characters, and an unpredictable ending.

Gullo, Jim
Trading Manny: How a Father and Son Learned to Love Baseball Again. 2012. Da Capo Press, ISBN 9780306820175. 255p. [Y][A]

Fathers and sons and baseball; does anyone want to read another book about this most often written about cliché? Maybe not, but some of us don't get tired of a good thing. This is a story of how a father and a son recaptured their love of baseball in an era of disillusionment due to steroids. They did it by removing the cards from their collection of known users and coming to the difficult understanding that sometimes our heroes are quite flawed human beings.

Jamieson, David
▶ *Mint Condition: How Baseball Cards Became an American Obsession.* 2010. Atlantic Monthly Press, ISBN 9780802119391. 272p.

Author Jamieson presents a compelling history of the American obsession with baseball cards. Find out how Topps came to dominate the baseball card industry after World War II and how the combination of chewing gum and baseball cards hooked an entire generation on the idea that collecting cards was cool. From flipping them to trading them, what kid growing up in America didn't go through a baseball card phase? I know I did. ★

Kiraly, Sherwood

📽 *Diminished Capacity.* 2008 (1995). St. Martin's Griffin, ISBN 9780312387037. 246p.

An extremely humorous novel about an unlikely trio who hatch a plan to sell a rare baseball card. Cooper Zerbs and his Uncle Rollie discover more than they bargained for as they travel to Chicago to a baseball memorabilia convention. Nothing earth-shattering here, but a clever, quick read that will leave you wanting more. Made into a movie with Alan Alda and Matthew Broderick.

Platt, Jim, James Buckley Jr., Franco Harris, and Maurice Lucas

Sports Immortals: Stories of Inspiration and Achievement. 2002. Triumph Books, ISBN 9781572434600. 180p.

Platt began collecting sports memorabilia over 50 years ago and much of his collection is on display at his Sports Immortals Museum in Boca Raton, Florida. This coffee table book features some of the top collectibles from the museum. What lends the book even more weight are the stories that accompany the pictures. Athletes include Jesse Owens, Muhammad Ali, Cy Young, and many others.

Wilker, Josh

Cardboard Gods: An All-American Tale. 2010. Seven Footer Press, ISBN 9781934734162. 243p. [Y][A]

For a lonely kid growing up in the 1970s, baseball cards became Wilker's lifeline. Anchored by players of the time like Tom Seaver, Wade Boggs, and Mark Fidrych, this memoir vividly captures the stages of growth in a boy's life while also reflecting the times of his childhood. Follow Wilker as he recalls a rather unconventional upbringing and the solace and happiness he found in slim packs of cards with a powdery stick of gum included.

Wong, Stephen

Smithsonian Baseball: Inside the World's Finest Private Collections. 2005. Smithsonian Books, ISBN 9780061121210. 286p.

This book captures our national pastime's history through the description and display of the best private collections in baseball memorabilia. Certainly, this will appeal to most baseball fans but also to those interested in American history or culture. It would also make a great gift for the baseball enthusiast in your family. ★

Stay Tuned—Media and Sports

Our memories of sports events extend beyond the games we have attended. As special as these may be, it is just as easy to recall those that we have watched on television or listened to on the radio. From the Olympic Games to the Super Bowl, we have gathered in groups or sat alone and immersed ourselves in the events as if we were there. This list of books reminds us of how important the television has become in our sports experiences. One radio book is included that focuses on our national obsession with sports talk radio.

Denninger, Dennis
Sports on Television: The How and Why Behind What You See. 2012. Routledge, ISBN 9780415896764. 248p.

>Deninger takes the reader through every aspect of sports as we watch it on television: from its simple beginnings to its rich and complex present, behind cameras, and inside boardrooms, explaining everything from TV rights to TV wrongs. It is a fine guidebook for anyone who wishes to understand the many-layered dimensions and decisions that shape and affect how sports comes through the screen and into our homes. As a longtime producer at ESPN, the author has the background needed to make this an accessible and rewarding read.

Garner, Joe
▶ *And the Fans Roared with 2 CDs: Recapture the Excitement of Great Moments in Sports*. 2002. Sourcebooks MediaFusion, ISBN 9781402200304. 192p.

>Forty unforgettable moments in sports history in pictures and sound remind us how television has made it possible for viewers to become part of those moments. Showcasing significant and iconic athletes such as Babe Ruth, Florence Griffith-Joyner, and notorious Mike Tyson, we revisit famous (and infamous) episodes. The book is a companion to the earlier title *And the Crowd Goes Wild* published in 1999.

Hyatt, Wesley
Kicking Off the Week: A History of Monday Night Football on ABC Television, 1970–2005. 2007. McFarland & Company, ISBN 9780786429691. 194p.

>Monday Night Football (MNF) !!!! Say it and excitement begins to build for the week's coming game, no matter who is playing. Well, now we have Sunday Night Football and Thursday Night Football and college football practically every night of the week. But once a upon a time, in 1970, when the Cleveland Browns opened the season against the New York Jets, this was all there was. Hyatt's book takes us back to the time before MNF began, setting the stage for its debut and following its reign on ABC television. From Frank Gifford and "Dandy" Don Meredith with Howard Cosell to the final curtain in 2005, this book will bring back memories for all "older" football fans.

Lawrence, Kelli
Skating on Air: The Broadcasting History of an Olympic Marquee Sport.
2011. McFarland & Co., ISBN 9780786446087. 234p.

Ever wonder why it seems like the Winter Olympic Games prime time television coverage is consumed with figure skating? This book tries to answer that and many other questions as it traces the rise in popularity of figure skating, and how much of it was due to its increased coverage on television. The book includes interviews with many commentators, skaters, producers, directors, and others. From Sonja Henie in the 1920s and 1930s to the scandals of 1994 and 2002, Lawrence illuminates and examines the broadcasting history of a beloved sport.

Miller, James Andrew and Tom Shales
Those Guys Have All the Fun: Inside the World of ESPN. 2011. Back Bay Books, ISBN 9780316043007. 763p. Y A

What began in 1979 as local sports cable channel in Connecticut is now arguably the most successful network in television history. The behind the scenes action is as entertaining as watching a good sporting event. Lots of gossip, backstabbing, and general mayhem make up much of the detail in the book. The authors interviewed most of the on-screen and backstage personalities who have been part of ESPN's fabulous success story. For all the couch potatoes out there, as well as those interested in the business of sport.

Ross, Betsy
Playing Ball with the Boys: The Rise of Women in the World of Men's Sports.
2010. Clerisy Press, ISBN 9781578604609. 191p.

Ross, former anchor for ESPN and still a television sports reporter, gives us a detailed history of women broadcasters in men's sports. Featuring interviews with athletes Billie Jean King and Rebecca Lobo, in addition to current women working in the media, Ross delineates women's slow encroachment into a male-dominated field.

The Thrill of Mystery

We searched for an original way to organize a mystery list but found that sports is a standard category for many books, websites, and databases. *Read on . . . Crime Fiction* has sports categories, as does sites like GoodReads.com and others. For example, below are two Massachusetts library sites that list authors by sport:

http://www.wakefieldlibrary.org/lists/zrasportssmys.htm
http://www.stonehamlibrary.org/sports.pdf

We tried to take a sample of notable mysteries with well-defined characters, interesting plotlines, and superior dialogue in order to present a general all-star lineup of sports themed who-done-its.

Brown, Jeremy

Suckerpunch: Book One in the Woodshed Wallace Series. 2011. Medallion Press, ISBN 9781605422251. 323p.

With staccato like rhythm reminiscent of Raymond Chandler, Brown takes readers into the world of MMA fighting. Aaron "Woodshed" Wallace, a local fighter, has an opportunity to break into the big time and make some real money. Unfortunately, the kidnapping of his friend by an unsavory bookie and the disappearance of his girlfriend complicate the story and Wallace has only hours to find her and make it to his fight. Numerous plot twists, frenetic action, and a colorful setting make for a thrilling ride. First book in the Woodshed Wallace series.

Coben, Harlan

Deal Breaker: The First Myron Bolitar Novel. 2012 (2006). Dell, ISBN 9780345535153. 400p.

Stunning dialogue, engaging characters, and a whirlwind plot propel readers in this highly entertaining series. Myron Bolitar is a former pro basketball player turned sports agent whose clients are forever causing him trouble. Bolitar's star client, quarterback Christian Steele, has received a call from his fiancé, which is usually a happy occasion. However, it's problematic for Bolitar and Christian, as she was assumed to be dead.

Crombie, Deborah

No Mark upon Her. 2012. William Morrow, ISBN 9780061990618. 384p.

Superintendent Duncan Kinkaid and his wife Detective Inspector Gemma James investigate the suspicious death of a fellow officer and Olympic caliber rower, Rebecca Meredith, who seemingly drowned while training. This beautifully plotted, complex mystery offers an intimate look into the solitary life of single scull rowers and the competitiveness of the rowing culture. This is the 14th book in the Kinkaid/James series, but it reads well as a stand-alone novel. ★

Gruley, Bryan

Starvation Lake: A Mystery. 2009 (2008). Touchstone, ISBN 9781416563624. 370p.

Gus Carpenter returns to his Michigan hometown after losing his job as a journalist. Folks remember him as the goalie that allowed a goal in the state finals costing his team a championship. When his high school hockey coach and mentor turns up dead, Gus searches for the truth in this highly suspenseful first novel. Gruley presents not only an engaging mystery, but also portrays the tight-knit, small-town environment with clear detail. ★

Huston, Charlie

Caught Stealing: A Novel. 2005 (2004). Ballantine Books, ISBN 9780345464781. 288p.

His baseball career cut short by injury, Hank Thompson is perfectly happy bartending in a dive bar in lower Manhattan. His life is turned upside down when a friend asks him to watch his cat. Russian mobsters beat him mercilessly and it isn't until he recovers that he finds a key hidden in the cat carrier. Hank must find his friend and steer clear of the many characters trying to do him harm, all the while keeping tabs on his favorite baseball team. Elmore Leonard fans will enjoy Huston's crisp, witty dialogue and brisk pacing. First in a trilogy. ★

Kovacs, Ed

Storm Damage. 2011. Minotauar Books, ISBN 9780312581817. 307p.

Set in New Orleans five months after Hurricane Katrina, Cliff St. James scours the city when he is hired to investigate a strange missing persons case. A former cop, mixed martial arts coach, and private investigator, his fighting skills come in handy as he and his tenacious partner Sgt. Honey Baybee navigate the anarchy and mayhem of post-Katrina.

Roorbach, Bill

▶ *Life among Giants.* 2013. Algonquin Books, ISBN 9781616200763. 352p.

David Hochmeyer or "Lizard," as he is known, is a successful NFL football player and his sister Kate is a tennis star, but the death of their parents when Lizard was in high school has taken its toll on them. Told from Lizard's point of view, he looks back to the murders in 1970 and brings readers to the present, to an extravagant setting with strange and memorable characters as he attempts to uncover the truth. Part mystery, part coming-of-age story, part literary fiction, and ultimately readable. ★

Veron, J. Michael

The Greatest Player Who Never Lived. 2001 (2000). Broadway Books, ISBN 9780767907163. 288p.

Charlie Hunter is an intern at a firm where the famed 1920s golfer Bobby Jones once worked. Hunter uncovers some documents that links Bobby Jones to a young golfer named Beau Stedman who disappeared after allegations of murder. Hunter tries to unravel the mystery of Stedman's past and his obsession leads to unexpected conclusions. Veron crafts a superb legal thriller that intertwines golf, history, and murder. ★

Forgotten, Forlorn, and Misbegotten Teams and Leagues

Leagues have come and gone. Cities have had teams appear and as quickly disappear. What happened to them all? Why were they not successful? What was the impact of losing them on a city or region? What happened to the players? The books in this category answer these questions and more.

Dunkel, Tom
Color Blind: The Forgotten Team That Broke Baseball's Color Line. 2013.
Atlantic Monthly Press, ISBN 9780802120120. 368p.

Before Jackie Robinson and after the Civil War, when baseball swept America, independent, semipro, and municipal leagues sprouted up everywhere. This is the story of drought-stricken Bismarck, North Dakota, and a remarkable team assembled by a quite unlikely champion. The team consisted of an even mix of black and white players and surprised many by winning the national semipro championship, mainly due to the presence of Satchel Paige, one of the greatest pitchers of all time. A remarkable story that warrants the attention of serious fans of baseball history. ★

Fosty, George and Darril Fosty
Black Ice: The Lost History of the Colored Hockey League of the Maritimes, 1895–1925. 2008 (2004). Nimbus Pub. Ltd., ISBN 9781551096957. 264p.

This practically forgotten hockey story is about the Colored Hockey League of the Maritimes, which began play in 1895 in Halifax, Nova Scotia. The authors argue (quite vehemently) that these black hockey players were actually the pioneers of what eventually became the National Hockey League, which wasn't officially organized until 1917. And that many of the rules and style of play were also hijacked by the NHL and taken as their own. An engaging account of a true "lost history."

Kurtzberg, Brad
Shorthanded: The Untold Story of the Seals: Hockey's Most Colorful Team. 2006. AuthorHouse, ISBN 9781425910280. 336p.

The Oakland/California Seals joined the NHL in 1967 at a time when the league believed expansion was the quickest way to financial success. The team stayed in the Bay Area for close to 10 years but never fully established a foothold. Part of the reason was the constantly changing ownership. Kurtzberg's book takes us behind the scenes of this particular franchise as an example of the dubious management practices that kept the NHL from reaching its potential until many years later. Players and coaches tell their own story as more than 110 interviews were conducted with former Seals players, owners, coaches, and employees.

Nelson, Murray
Abe Saperstein and the American Basketball League, 1960–1963: The Upstarts Who Shot for Three and Lost to the NBA. 2013. McFarland, ISBN 9780786472444. 220p.

A long-forgotten league that in its two short years of existence was responsible for innovations that are still used in today's NBA, including the wider lane, 30-second clock, and 3-point shot. It also broke the color line by hiring the first African American head coach. In addition, George Steinbrenner owned his first team in this league. Saperstein was its colorful commissioner and was also responsible for founding the team that became known as the Harlem Globetrotters.

Pluto, Terry
▶ *Loose Balls: The Short, Wild Life of the American Basketball Association.* 2007. Simon and Schuster, ISBN 9780671673901. 450p. ⛾Ⓨ⛾Ⓐ

   The American Basketball Association (ABA) came into existence beginning in 1967 and over the next nine seasons attempted to compete with the more established National Basketball Association. The ABA hoped to attract fans who were not easily able to attend NBA games. Julius Erving, Connie Hawkins, George Gervin, and Moses Malone were just a few of the stars who began their careers in the ABA. Pluto interviews many of the participants and even some of the fans who attended the games. A fun read that blends pro basketball history with lots of humor. ★

Speck, Mark
. . . And a Dollar Short: The Empty Promises, Broken Dreams, and Somewhat-Less-Than-Comic Misadventures of the 1974 Florida Blazers. 2011. Saint Johann Press, ISBN 9781878282774. 278p.

   The World Football League was only in existence for two years and this book tells the story of one of those ill-fated franchises. In its short life, what became the Florida Blazers changed owners, cities, and even names numerous times before they played their first game. Their city didn't really want them. Their fans didn't really care. Despite it all, they went on to win a division title. This is their story.

West, Gary
Kentucky Colonels of the American Basketball Association: The Real Story of a Team Left Behind. 2011. Acclaim Press, ISBN 9781935001829. 352p.

   One of the ABA's most successful teams, the Kentucky Colonels featured ABA stars Dan Issel and Artis Gilmore. Some believe they could have competed for an NBA title. Written with the help of Lloyd "Pink" Gardner who played for the Colonels, West's book tells the story of this long-forgotten team, its owners, players, and the city of Louisville itself.

Willes, Ed
The Rebel League: The Short and Unruly Life of the World Hockey Association. 2005. McClelland & Stewart, ISBN 9780771089497. 288p.

   Talk about wild. The World Hockey Association that operated between 1972 and 1979 and challenged the supremacy of the National Hockey League fits the bill. They hoped to compete by paying the players more. When Bobby Hull, one of the top NHL players jumped leagues, a lot more fans began to take them seriously. Willes details how this one act changed the course of the NHL by freeing players from the reserve clause, which allowed them move to other teams via free agency. It also helped the league expand into the south and paved the way for an influx of European players.

Chapter Three

Setting

In sports, the appeal of setting may come in various forms. Think of the Super Bowl or the Kentucky Derby. It is the appeal of the spectacle as much as the game or race. People attend or watch because of the "where" as much as the "whom." Now think of the Olympics or mountain climbing or rowing. The settings are part of the attraction. From *Road Trips* to some of the *Most Dangerous Sports*, these categories appeal to us because they are either set in beautiful locales or because they take place in a world outside of the games or matches.

Fantasy Leagues

While many of us love sports, are obsessed with them, and spend too much time watching them, it is a fact that very few of us can actually play the games very well. So at some point, it wasn't enough to be just a passive spectator. It began with board games in the 1950s and 1960s and eventually morphed into the fantasy games that are all the rage today. This list will take you through the best of those that illuminate or help justify these obsessions.

Barmack, Eric and Max Handelman
Why Fantasy Football Matters: And Our Lives Do Not. 2006. Gallery Books, ISBN 9781416909965. 256p.

A way into the psyche of fantasy football fanatics for those with no real interest in the subject, this easy to follow, hilarious book gives loads of insight into why people are hooked on fantasy sports. It also provides some very worthwhile advice on how to compete at a high level in your own league. As someone who played fantasy football for many years, I could have used some help.

Coover, Robert
The Universal Baseball Association, Inc., J. Henry Waugh, Prop. 2011 (1968). Overlook, ISBN 9781590203118. 256p.

    Considered by some to be the best baseball novel ever written, Coover's book has a protagonist whose fantasy players exist only in his mind. Part mystery, part fantasy, always darkly comic, this is also the first book to suggest a fantasy league as a way to escape from real life. ★

Gray, Scott
The Mind of Bill James. 2006. Doubleday, ISBN 9780385514644. 256p.

    Bill James is the father of Sabermetrics, which is the "specialized analysis of baseball through objective evidence, especially baseball statistics that measure in-game activity" (Ask.com). It is said that this has changed the way many of us view the game. His yearly baseball books in the 1980s and 1990s (*The Baseball Abstract* and *The Baseball Book*) coincided with the rise in popularity of fantasy baseball and I can say with firsthand knowledge that his books were THE main source fantasy players used to give them that added edge and confidence. Many major league teams have since utilized his uses of statistics and James himself was brought in to help analyze players for the Boston Red Sox, which some say partially accounted for them ending their long-standing World Series drought. Gray's book chronicles the life and ideas of James and will appeal to any baseball fan who loves to study box scores or any student of the game.

Mass, A. J.
How Fantasy Sports Explains the World: What Pujols and Peyton Can Teach Us about Wookies and Wall Street. 2011. Skyhorse Publishing, ISBN 9781620876039. 256p.

    Mass is a fantasy sports expert for ESPN and has learned that people take what he says very seriously. He has also learned that the same skills used in evaluating fantasy sports talent are similar to what is used in everyday life. He gives examples from throughout history to prove his point in this entertaining and informative book.

St. Amant, Mark
Committed: Confessions of a Fantasy Football Junkie. 2005. Scribner, ISBN 9780743267564. 304p.

    Fantasy football, like other fantasy sports, uses statistics from actual games and players to determine winners and losers. Via the Internet, it has grown into a phenomenon. St. Amant somehow convinced his wife to let him quit his day job to pursue a fantasy football title. His pursuit of that title is the main thrust of the book, along with a good dose of history and self-deprecating humor.

Walker, Sam
▶ *Fantasy Land: A Season on Baseball's Lunatic Fringe.* 2006. Viking, ISBN 9780670034284. 368p.

Walker is a sportswriter for the *Wall Street Journal*, and he decided to take a closer look at this growing obsession by immersing himself in a season of fantasy baseball. Unlike most enthusiasts, he had access to in-person visits to spring training camps to prepare for his draft. In this sense he is not typical. Told with humor, skepticism, and a keen eye for the absurd. ★

Off the Beaten Path—Unlikely Pastimes That Pass for Sport

A basic definition of sport is "an athletic activity requiring skill or physical prowess and often of a competitive nature" (dictionary.com). That definition is pretty broad and we will use it here to encompass some of the odd or less mainstream sports that maybe us schlubs can play or do. Well, probably not but decide for yourself with these books.

Bilger, Burkhard
Noodling for Flatheads: Moonshine, Monster Catfish and Other Southern Comforts. 2000. Scribner, ISBN 9780684850115. 256p.

In a category of unlikely pastimes, Bilger chronicles a few "games" that will have you scratching your head (not included here but . . .). Cockfighting, moonshining, and rolley hole (played with marbles) are just a few as Bilger travels from West Virginia to Oklahoma and treats the games and players with grace and respect. They might end up with our respect also.

Cross, Shauna
▪ *Derby Girl.* 2007. Henry Holt and Co., ISBN 9780805080230. 234p. [Y][A]

Made into the movie *Whip It*, Cross's novel describes the wild world of roller derby rolled into a coming-of-age story. It follows main character, high school misfit Bliss Cavendar, as she discovers roller derby helps her into a world that accepts her and is able to embrace as her own. It's a good story that sheds light onto a sport that has gained in popularity.

Fagone, Jason
Horsemen of the Esophagus: Competitive Eating and the Big Fat American Dream. 2006. Broadway, ISBN 9780307237392. 320p.

Great title, don't you think? What's more American than a competition for those who like to eat prodigiously? Fagone travels to 27 eating contests over 2 continents and leaves us with a mouthful of information to digest. It's far easier than eating 50 hot dogs in 12 minutes at Coney Island, which is what legendary Takeru Kobayashi did. Hold the mustard and enjoy the book.

Fatsis, Stephan

Word Freak: Heartbreak, Triumph, Genius and Obsession in the World of Competitive Scrabble Players. 2002. Penguin Books, ISBN 9780142002261. 416p.

> Here's an off-the-beaten-path sport that most of us can relate to. Since its invention in the 1930s, Scrabble has been a favorite among families, mixing fun and a chance to expand one's vocabulary. Fatsis takes us into the psychology and physiology of the competitive Scrabble player and turns into a pretty good player himself in the process.

Fontova, Umberto

The Helldivers' Rodeo: A Deadly, X-Treme, Scuba-Diving, Spearfishing, Adventure amid the Offshore Oil Platforms in the Murky Waters of the Gulf of Mexico. 2001. M. Evans & Co., ISBN 9780871319364. 244p.

> The danger involved in spearfishing beneath oilrigs is difficult to comprehend. Huge fish, dives to over 200 feet, and shaky equipment are all part of the fun for this odd assortment of characters. A fast-paced, sometimes thrilling account of Cuban-born Fontova's adventures tagging along in the waters around the oilrigs in the Gulf of Mexico.

Grant, Steve

Ping Pong Fever: The Madness That Swept 1902 America. 2012. CreateSpace, ISBN 9781475018608. 268p.

> Ping pong (or table tennis as it's known internationally) is one of the most popular sports played throughout the world. It has been an Olympic sport since 1988. Ping pong was introduced to America in 1902 and took the country by storm. Grant takes us back to that year through text and photographs, and for anyone who had a table in their basement (I did), this book comes highly recommended.

Lorr, Benjamin

▶ *Hell-Bent: Obsession, Pain, and the Search for Something Like Transcendence in Competitive Yoga.* 2012. St. Martin's Press, ISBN 9780312672904. 320p.

> Who knew there was a form of yoga considered extreme? Not me, but Bikram's yoga classes run for 90 minutes and are practiced in a room heated to 105°F. Notable practitioners include Lady Gaga, Kobe Bryant, and Madonna. Lorr walked into a yoga studio on a whim and came out a believer. He chronicles remarkable transformations including his own. ★

Pasquale, Anthony Leonardo and Cade Beaulieu, illustrator.

Ultimate: The Greatest Sport Ever Invented by Man. 2008. Breakaway Books, ISBN 9781891369759. 148p.

> So for you novices out there, Ultimate is a game played with a flying disc (known by many and most often referred to as a "Frisbee"). The sport is a kind of offshoot of American football as the object is to advance the disc by

throwing and catching it until your team reaches an opponent's end zone. It is very popular on college campuses and is often played intramurally. The book doesn't take itself too seriously while providing enough details to keep neophytes interested and even the avid player amused.

Rosen, Michael
No Dribbling the Squid: Octopus, Shin-Kicking, Elephant Polo, and Other Oddball Sports. 2009. Andrews McNeel Publishing, ISBN 9780740781209. 240p.

An easy book to pick up and browse, the sheer variety of sports described is thoroughly entertaining and mystifying. Not to be confused with a traditional narrative, Rosen provides plenty of pictures to enhance the experience of learning about sports only a person of great imagination could fathom.

It's a Business, Not a Game

Professional sports revenues alone are over 30 billion dollars (Hoover's. com). It can be hard for fans to relate to some athletes' salaries, as most of us would be in heaven to pitch or hit in front of 30,000 spectators. Athletes may be resented for making millions of dollars to play games many of us played as children. There are those who have become so disgusted with player salaries that they have stopped supporting professional sports. Here we consider titles that break down money and sports and offer insight into the economics of the games.

Berri, David J. and Martin Schmidt
Stumbling On Wins: Two Economists Expose the Pitfalls on the Road to Victory in Professional Sports. 2010. FT Press, ISBN 9780132357784. 256p.

The authors make the point that if sports teams, who have so much athlete information at their disposal, get it wrong so often, what chance do regular human beings have to make the right decisions in life? The goal here is to understand and improve the decisions made by sports teams and to increase their success rate. Some very interesting hypotheses are presented, appealing to those who look at things from an analytical viewpoint.

Helyar, John
The Lords of the Realm. 1995 (1994). Ballantine Books, ISBN 9780345392619. 632p.

This is a history of baseball for those who really want to know the truth about the game. Meticulously researched and accessibly written, Helyar's book looks back at the business of baseball from its early days up until the mid-1990s. Details on strikes in later years and owner's lowballing offers to star players in days gone by are presented with brutal honesty. The book spotlights game changer Marvin Miller who after years of trying finally convinced the players that an organized union was the only way they could overturn the reserve clause, which prohibited player movement and upon its removal would eventually result in the dramatic rise in salaries that exist today.

Hyman, Mark

The Most Expensive Game in Town: The Rising Cost of Youth Sports and the Toll on Today's Families. 2012. Beacon Press, ISBN 9780807001448. 160p.

Our obsession with youth sports and the costs associated with it are getting way out of hand. It not only drains our financial resources, but also exacts a mental toll that is hard to fathom. Hyman presents hard facts in a readable, nonjudgmental way so that we can see how far off the deep end some parents and communities have fallen.

Lewis, Michael

▶ 🎞 ***Moneyball: The Art of Winning an Unfair Game.*** 2004 (2003). W. W. Norton and Company, ISBN 9780393324815. 320p.

One of the most popular books ever written on the business of sport, *Moneyball* looks at the Oakland A's baseball franchise and ponders how one of the teams with the lowest player salaries competed so well at the beginning of the new century. The story revolves around general manager Billy Beane and how he employs statistics not used by other GMs to evaluate players (see Bill James and Sabermetrics) and thus get useful talent for relatively meager salaries. This system has paid big dividends for him over the years and has now influenced other teams in the way they evaluate and acquire players. ★

Luchs, John

Illegal Procedure: A Sports Agent Comes Clean on the Dirty Business of College Sport. 2012. Bloomsbury, ISBN 9781608197217. 288p.

A troubling, enlightening indictment of big-time college sports, Luchs's life as a sports agent turned reformer is an eye-opening account of college sports gone awry. He details some of the painful truths he encountered during his career, but what's amazing is how little things have changed.

Mauboussin, Michael

The Success Equation: Untangling Skill and Luck in Business, Sports, and Investing. 2012. Harvard Business Review Press, ISBN 9781422184233. 320p.

A popular math book—wait, is that possible? For fans of *Moneyball*, Mauboussin's book looks at skill and luck and how this combination might lead to success in leadership, sports, and investing. An enjoyable read that is accessible from beyond a business standpoint.

Smit, Barbara

Sneaker Wars: The Enemy Brothers Who Founded Adidas and Puma and the Family Feud That Forever Changed the Business of Sports. 2008. Harper, ISBN 9780061246586. 400p.

Who knew the founders of what would become the beginnings of the battle for sneaker supremacy were Bavarian brothers? And that their falling out would lead to the creation of two companies that began the global fight for the sneaker market? Smit's book gives us the backstory involved in this evolution and explains why tennis shoes have become as much status symbol as functional feet warmers.

Sperber, Murray
Beer and Circus: How Big Time College Sports Is Crippling Undergraduate Education. 2000. Henry Holt and Company, ISBN 9780805038644. 288p.

Sperber looks at the connection between the cost of intercollegiate athletics and undergraduate education focusing mainly on large public universities. He makes the case that because so much money is spent on athletics and research, there is little left for the typical student, so administrators perpetuate the party atmosphere, which surrounds college sports to keep these students happy. While the book is over 10 years old, the hypothesis is even more relevant today. ★

The Most Dangerous Sports

Some people have to live on the edge. Bridge or crochet is not their thing. So they seek out the more extreme sports. This list is made up of books that feature sports that challenge in most unusual ways. Enjoy from a distance.

Cannell, Michael
The Limit: Life and Death on the 1961 Grand Prix Circuit. 2011. Twelve, ISBN 9780446554732. 336p.

Reading more like a novel, this is the enthralling story of Phil Hill and his pinnacle year on the Grand Prix circuit, 1961. From his early life as a mechanic in California to become the first American to win the Grand Prix, you'll want to have your seat belt fastened (which didn't exist at the time) for this dangerous ride.

Casey, Susan
The Wave: In Pursuit of the Rogues, Freaks, and Giants of the Ocean. 2007. Anchor, ISBN 9780767928854. 432p.

The author takes us in search of the largest waves in the oceans of the world. According to Casey, the waves are ground shattering, terrifying, and fascinating to observe. Surfers and scientists alike are obsessed with them. As she travels the world, she experiences up close the dangers that are presented by these most impressive waves.

Hemingway, Ernest
Death in the Afternoon. 1996 (1932). Scribner, ISBN 9780684801452. 496p. [Y][A]

Master storyteller Hemingway is at his best when describing the fine art of bullfighting. Part history, part spectacle, this classic from 1932 is still considered "the" book on the subject. While devoting much time to the technical details of the sport, Hemingway comments on what it takes to put oneself in real danger every time bullfighters practice their sport. He also talks at length on the art of writing and how bullfighting sparks his imagination.

Hyde, Elizabeth

In the Heart of the Canyon. 2009. Vintage, ISBN 9780307276421. 336p.

A novel about rafting through the Grand Canyon that creates believable characters into a riveting story. During the course of the 13-day trip, the passengers and rafting guides come to know each other more intimately than they could have imagined. The experiences both physically and emotionally will last a lifetime. Detailed descriptions of the canyon and rapids make the story quite believable. ★

Peter, Josh

Fried Twinkies, Buckle Bunnies, & Bull Riders: A Year Inside the Professional Bull Riders Tour. 2005. Rodale Books, ISBN 9781594865220. 272p.

Not for the faint of heart, bull riding is for most a low-reward, high-risk endeavor. Peter's book takes us behind the scenes and focuses on defending champion Justin McBride as he finds out how hard it is to stay on top. Broken bones and groupies are just two of the perks of this sport. ★

Ralston, Aron

📖 *127 Hours: Between a Rock and a Hard Place.* 2010 (2004). Atria Books, ISBN 9780743492812. 354p. Ⓨ Ⓐ

Known more for the movie starring James Franco, the book is an engrossing account of Ralston's imprisonment (127 hours) between rock formations while mountain climbing in Utah. Although an experienced climber, Ralston had no idea what this hike had in store, making it unforgettable for him and for us.

Ramo, Joshua Cooper

No Visible Horizon: Surviving the World's Most Dangerous Sport. 2003. Simon & Schuster, ISBN 9780743257909. 288p.

Think "air show" and you'll have an idea what this book is about. Known as aerial acrobatics, this sport will appeal to those who enjoy the beauty and danger inherent in flying planes through figures in the sky. Ramo is a flyer himself and he'll have you reeling from the in-depth descriptions of the sport.

Tabor, James M.

▶ *Blind Descent: The Quest to Discover the Deepest Place on Earth.* 2010. Constable, ISBN 9781849018562. 320p.

Caving? Really? Look it up!—It exists. Tabor presents accounts of the obstacles that must be overcome in deep-cave exploration. The book focuses on two cavers, an American and a Russian, as they attempt to penetrate supercaves. Beautifully detailed and highly informative, the book will captivate you in totally unexpected ways. ★

Outdoor Life—Nature and Sport

Not all sports are about winning and losing. Some give us time to reflect or compete while immersed in the beauty of gentle waters or divine forests. The following titles are more about the beauty of nature and the sports that take place there.

Clark, Michael
Digital Masters: Adventure Photography: Capturing the World of Outdoor Sports. 2010. Lark Books, ISBN 9781600595196. 224p.

A lovely photography book that focuses on adventure and extreme sports, it is also of interest to those who dabble in photography as a hobby as it includes numerous tips and ideas for shooting outdoors. Includes photos of mountain biking, surfing, and ice climbing.

Colegate, Isabel
The Shooting Party. 2010 (1981). Counterpoint, ISBN 9781582435930. 208p.

An astute portrayal of English nobility on the cusp of World War I before the world changed forever. Set at a lovely English estate, Sir Randolph Nettleby invites a host of characters over for a weekend shoot and as they converse and interact, we get a sense of their attitudes and prejudices. Colgate is sparse with her prose and transports us back to a time and place that seems more like ancient history than just a century ago.

Duncan, David James
▬ *The River Why.* 2002 (1982). Sierra Club Books, ISBN 9781578050840. 304p. Ⓨ Ⓐ

A novel about fly-fishing, but really this is a coming-of-age tale that captivates the reader with its wit and irreverence. A young man decides to leave his fishing obsessed family and strike out on his own. Along the way, he learns more about himself and life than he expected. Wonderfully written and filled with captivating, quirky characters, Duncan's book will leave you longing for your own outdoors adventure.

Miller, David
AWOL on the Appalachian Trail. 2011. Mariner Books, ISBN 9780547745527. 352p.

Author Miller decided he would like to hike the complete Appalachian Trail as a kind of gift to himself before he settles in as an adult for the rest of his life; so in 2003, he took a leave from his job and family to do so. He describes the journey in vivid detail and allows readers to feel like they are a part of the adventure. For those so inspired to follow suit, there are many tips on preparing for a successful hike.

Strayed, Cheryl
▶ *Wild.* 2011. Knopf, ISBN 9780307592736. 336p.

Strayed's book on her experience hiking the Pacific Crest Trail (PCT) is more about her life and what led her to this journey than the hike itself. And while there is plenty of information on the particulars of hiking, we also learn about the events that brought her to this moment in time. Along the way, we share the challenges she faces and discover what makes the PCT so unique. Chosen by Oprah as a book club selection, it lends itself particularly well to discussion. Hailed as one of the best books of 2012 by *Entertainment Weekly*, NPR, and *The Boston Globe*. ★

Walton, Izaak
The Compleat Angler. 2011 (1653). CreateSpace Independent Publishing Platform, ISBN 9781463702106. 164p.

No book celebrates outdoor sport and fishing like this classic from 360 years ago. As much philosophy as fishing, filled with humor and anecdotes, let these words take you back to a simpler, more charming time. And for those so inclined, you might discover some invaluable tips on fly-fishing too.

Road Trips—Traveling and Sports

Sometimes it's not enough to sit at home watching our favorite sports. Some say there is nothing like being at a live sports event. The road trip is half the fun. The other half is the live event itself. Here are some books that should get you itching to fill up the old gas-guzzler and take to the open road.

Coyne, Tom
A Course Called Ireland: A Long Walk in Search of a Country, a Pint, and the Next Tee. 2009. Gotham Books, ISBN 9781592404247. 311p.

A "failed" golfer (Coyne did not qualify for the PGA tour but he wrote a book about it, *Paper Tiger*) is approaching fatherhood and decides to take the golfing trip of a lifetime to Ireland—home to some of the most beautiful golf courses in the world. Coyne made the entire coast of Ireland his golf links, walking from course to course around the circumference of the country. An insightful laugh-out-loud travelogue that familiarizes us as much with pubs as golf courses.

Oxenham, Gwendolyn
Finding the Game: Three Years, Twenty-five Countries, and the Search for Pickup Soccer. 2012. St. Martin's Press, ISBN 9781250002044. 288p.

When the women's professional soccer league went under, Oxenham found herself at a crossroads. She was 23 and a former star player for Duke

University. Her life had revolved around the game and she wasn't ready to give it up. The result was her decision to travel the world and document pickup soccer games for a film and this book is the result of that pursuit. Her love of soccer in its purest form and the people she meets make this appeal to nonsports fans as well as travel buffs with an eye toward the adventurous.

Posnanski, Joe 🏆

▶ *The Soul of Baseball: A Road Trip through Buck O'Neil's America.* 2007. William Morrow, ISBN 9780060854034. 288p.

Legendary Negro League player and a member of the Baseball Hall of Fame Buck O'Neil spent part of the last year of his life traveling with author Posnanski to some of the cities where he played ball. Of special interest is their stop in Kansas City where O'Neil played for the Monarchs. Memories are stirred of the people and cities he got to know along the way, but most of all, we get to meet the man who just happened to be a ballplayer. An endearing, loving, and inspirational portrait written with great tenderness. ★

Rushin, Steve

Road Swing: One Fan's Journey into the Soul of America's Sports. 1998. Main Street Books, ISBN 9780385483926. 256p.

As author Rushin closed in on his 30th birthday, he found himself eager to attempt a road trip that would allow him to indulge his lifelong obsession with sports. The result of that enviable trip is this book. He visits Iowa to see the famous "Field of Dreams" and Indiana to see where Larry Bird grew up. Never taking himself too seriously, Rushin's tale is told with great humor and a real awareness of his good fortune to be able to do this.

Tuchman, Robert

The 100 Sporting Events You Must See Live: An Insider's Guide to Creating the Sports Experience of a Lifetime. 2009. BenBella Books, ISBN 9781933771458. 337p.

For the sports fan that has everything, Tuchman provides information on traveling to the greatest sporting events around the world. The Masters, World Cup, and Monaco Grand Prix are here along with the Calgary Stampede and Ironman World Championship. Histories of the events are provided and hotel rooms and restaurants are suggested for your trip. Combining sports history and magic moments, this travelogue can help you imagine getting out of your living room and experiencing a one of a kind sporting event.

Wolff, Alexander

Big Game, Small World. 2003 (2002). Grand Central Publishing, ISBN 9780446679893. 448p.

The author sets off on an international tour of 16 different nations and 8 states as he tracks the growth of basketball as a world sport. From Japan to Brazil, Wolff proves the games essence transcends national boundaries. Written with a light touch and constant humor, the book is a slam-dunk for basketball fans and also of interest to travel aficionados.

Out of This World—Sports in Speculative Fiction

Readers were enthralled and amazed by J. K. Rowling's portrayal of Quidditch, a high-flying fantastical sport; and *The Hunger Games* dramatic contest to the death captured the hearts and minds of both children and adults. These authors imagine the world of sports and athletes in settings of imagined worlds and possible futures. All of the titles in this category may appeal to young adult readers. Y

Cline, Ernest
Ready Player One. 2011. Crown, ISBN 9780307887436. 384p.
In 2044, the real world is a gritty, dark, and dangerous place. Lonely teenager Wade Watts (and most of humanity) chooses instead to spend his time in the virtual world of the OASIS. When it is revealed that there is an Easter egg "treasure" buried within this reality by its eccentric and deceased creator, millions join the hunt. Filled with references to 1980s pop culture and an adrenaline-fueled race to the end. Ok, this is a 1980s video game lover's book, so "sport" is a stretch, but we really liked it. ★

Collins, Suzanne
🎬 *The Hunger Games.* 2010 (2008). Scholastic Press, ISBN 9780439023528. 384p.
The first title in the trilogy of the same name, *The Hunger Games* shows Katniss fighting for her district and humanity, using her archery expertise, intelligence, and sympathy for her rivals in the live reality TV battle that can have only one survivor. This grim view of a future United States has wide appeal due to its likable and admirable heroine overcoming the odds stacked against her. ★

Dann, Jack and Gardner R. Dozois
Future Sports. 2002. Ace, ISBN 9780441009619. 272p.
A unique anthology of short science fiction stories presenting athletics of tomorrow. Some top-notch authors are represented including Arthur C. Clarke, Ian McDonald, and Jonathan Lethem. A couple border on fantasy but all imagine the future with familiar or newly created sports.

Gould, Stephen
Impulse. 2013. Tor Books, ISBN 9780765327574. 368p.
Teleportation and snowboarding collide in the third installment of the Jumper series. David and his wife can teleport and have tried to shield their daughter Cent from several groups that would like to use her for their own ends. If you think raising a teenager is tough, try controlling one that can leave at will. Some believe Gould is a direct heir to Robert A. Heinlein, which can't be a bad thing. Read for yourself and see.

Kosmatka, Ted
▶ *The Games*. 2012. Del Ray, ISBN 9780345526618. 368p.

In the future, an Olympic sport pits genetically mutated creatures against each other. One of the newest creations created by the USOC has begun to show a high level of intelligence that is only matched by its viciousness. As the final competition nears, scientist race to find what secrets are hidden in its DNA. As this action-packed thriller races to the end, questions are explored about the need for morality within science. Complex characters and a not-so-far-off near-future setting makes this a fun and disturbing read. ★

Parker, K. J.
Sharps. 2012. Orbit, ISBN 9780316177757. 480p.

A fencing team on a goodwill tour traverse Parker's fictitious medieval fantasy world. Combining political and military intrigue, the story is set in an imagined 17th century with sword fighting, assassinations, and a bit of humor. The fencers are often faced with long rides or downtime that makes chess games seem exciting. A great adventure that will appeal to those who prefer setting or character-driven stories.

Pratchett, Terry
Unseen Academicals. 2010 (2009). Harper, ISBN 9780061161728. 448p.

In the 37th book of the Discworld series, Pratchett combines football (soccer), fashion, and food along with the usual wizards in the fantasy realm. A gentle jibe at sports and its fans laced with plenty of humor and action. For language lovers too, Pratchett writes as clever as ever.

Sigler, Scott
The Rookie: Galactic Football League #1. 2007. Diversion Books, ISBN 9781938120091. 464p. [Y][A]

Set 700 years in the future, this exciting sports riff on space opera entertains with aliens, action, and intrigue. Quentin Barnes is a great player in the all-human purist National Football League (NFL) and he has been enlisted to the Ionath Krakens of the GFL to lead them as their new quarterback. Fueled by superb world building and an eccentric cast of characters, Sigler's imagining of future football is dark, lethal, and superbly entertaining.

The Olympics

From Athens to London, from 776 BC (first ancient Olympic Games) and 1896 (first modern Olympics) to London 2012, the Olympics have held our fascination through triumph and tragedy. This list takes us back and brings us current to all things Olympic.

Coffey, Wayne and Jim Craig
The Boys of Winter: The Untold Story of a Coach, a Dream, and the 1980 U.S. Olympic Hockey Team. 2005. Broadway, ISBN 9781400047666. 288p.

Another "where were you when" moment in Olympic and sports history. "Do you believe in miracles?" was sportscaster Al Michaels's call as the clock wound down in the gold medal hockey game in Lake Placid, New York, in 1980. Coffey offers a unique perspective on this watershed sports event when the U.S. amateurs took on a Russian hockey powerhouse. Driven by coach Herb Brooks who turned the players into a close-knit family, they captured the American imagination like few teams before or since. ★

Feinstein, John
Rush for the Gold: Mystery at the Olympics. 2012. Knopf, ISBN 9780375869631. 320p. Y A

Feinstein's books combine sports action, mystery, and behind-the-scenes glimpses of big-time sporting events. This one takes place at the 2012 Olympics in London and has recurring character Susan Carol Anderson as she competes in swimming events. Featuring actual Olympic athletes Michael Phelps and Ryan Lochte, this is a real page-turner and will appeal to young adults as well as adults.

Large, David Clay
Munich 1972: Tragedy, Terror, and Triumph at the Olympic Games. 2012. Rowan and Littlefield, ISBN 9780742567399. 396p.

Munich 1972 is both terrific sporting history and a gripping chronicle of the Black September terror attack that took the lives of 11 Israeli Olympians. For those old enough to remember this tragedy, it compares to the drama that unfolded around President Kennedy's assassination. The book reminds us of how politics have always played a part in the Olympic Games and how the importance we place on sports is easily overshadowed by tragic events.

Maranniss, David
Rome 1960: The Summer Olympics That Changed the World. 2008. Simon and Schuster, ISBN 9781416534075. 496p.

The Rome Olympics were not as flamboyant or tragic as others, but they did star Cassius Clay, Wilma Randolph, and barefoot Ethiopian marathoner Abebe Bikila. They had the first doping scandal and were the first Summer Games televised into our homes. A much simpler time . . . but times were changing. ★

McCallum, Jack
Dream Team: How Michael, Magic, Larry, Charles, and the Greatest Team of All Time Conquered the World and Changed the Game of Basketball Forever. 2012. Ballantine Books, ISBN 9780345520487. 384p. Y A

Why was the 1992 Olympic basketball team dubbed the "Dream Team"? Because four of the greatest basketball players of all-time were on it. Michael

Jordan, Magic Johnson, Larry Bird, and Charles Barkley captivated the world and remade the National Basketball Association into a global sensation. Mc-Cullum was with them from their first practice through the Olympic gold medal ceremony. He had unlimited access then and spoke to each in-depth 20 years later for this book. ★

Mullen, P. H.
▶ *Gold in the Water: The True Story of Ordinary Men and Their Extraordinary Dream of Olympic Glory.* 2003 (2001). St. Martin's Griffin. ISBN 9780312311162. 352p.

When we sit down to watch the Olympics, we are seeing the best athletes in their events. How do they get there? What does it take to make it? How much difference is there between those who qualify and those who don't? Mullen chronicles the lives of four young men as they strive to qualify for the U.S. swim team in Australia in 2000. This will appeal not just to swimmers but anyone who wonders what it takes to make it to the greatest stage in sports. ★

Perrottet, Tony
The Naked Olympics. 2004. Random House Trade, ISBN 9780812969917. 256p.

In featuring books on the Olympics, we must also take a look way back to keep in perspective how much the games have changed. Perrottet's book recreates the times as well as the games of ancient Greece and the festival he dubbed "the Woodstock of antiquity." These "games" unique events included beauty contests, fire-swallowers, and some scrumptious dining options such as roasted sow's womb. Wish we could have been there.

Woodland, Les
The Olympics' 50 Craziest Stories. 2011. McGann Publishing LLC, ISBN 9780984311781. 160p.

Even the most ardent of Olympic fans won't know more than a couple of these stories. A collection of fun, offbeat tales throughout Olympic history. Woodland is a cyclist himself, but in covering that sport, he obviously uncovered lots more that interested him in this less serious account of Olympics gone by.

1936—An Olympic Year

While doing research for this book, we have found that after deciding on a category, it is sometimes difficult to find the requisite six to eight titles that each category warrants. And at times, we have second-guessed some of our category selections. In the case of the 1936 Olympics, we were taken aback by so many "good to great" books, both fiction and nonfiction. While some may believe that two categories devoted to the Olympics is too much, we feel that the range in writing and mass popularity of the games make it a slam dunk. Without further ado . . .

Brown, Daniel James

The Boys in the Boat: Nine American and Their Quest for Gold at the 1936 Berlin Olympics. 2013. Viking, ISBN 9780670025817. 432p.

This is the epic saga of how the American rowing team advanced to become a surprise gold medal winner at the Berlin Olympic Games. We meet Joe Rantz and the other boys in the boat at the beginning of their freshman year at the University of Washington in 1933. We follow them through each year of rowing, leading up to the 1936 Olympics, and the author provides significant detail regarding the art of rowing and the construction of the racing boats. Brown blends personal recollections and newspaper accounts skillfully and builds up the suspense as the race draws near. Talk about overcoming the odds; these boys did it! ★

Deaver, Jeffrey

Garden of Beasts: A Novel of Berlin. 2005 (2004). Pocket Star, ISBN 9780743437820. 576p.

A hired killer (Paul Schumann) caught by the authorities agrees to travel to Hitler's Berlin on the eve of the 1936 Olympics to assassinate Germany's "rearmament tsar" Reinhard Ernst in an attempt to halt Hitler's rise to power. When Schumann arrives in Berlin along with the U.S. Olympic team, he meets his contact and sets out to plan his kill. Deaver's story is quite unpredictable and will satisfy his many fans in addition to many others. Not Lincoln Rhyme, but the book has all of Deaver's talents on display.

Deford, Frank

Bliss Remembered. 2011. Overlook TP, ISBN 9781590206423. 352p.

Deford, a longtime columnist for *Sports Illustrated* and an NPR commentator, spins a story that blends romance, historical fiction, intrigue, and a commentary on the Great Depression and World War II as seen through the eyes of an old woman recalling her youth. The woman, Sidney Stringfellow Branch, is dying of cancer and wants to tell her son the story of her youth, a story she has kept secret for all these years. As an American swimmer arriving in Berlin for the 1936 Olympics, the last thing she expected was to fall in love with a German officer. This finely crafted novel will appeal specifically to readers who enjoy historical fiction. ★

Frei, Terri

Olympic Affair: A Novel of Hitler's Siren and America's Hero. 2012. Taylor Trade Publishing, ISBN 9781589796980. 336p.

This novel imagines the affair between Glenn Morris, the American decathlon winner in the 1936 Berlin Olympics, and Leni Riefenstahl, a German filmmaker and actress known as Hitler's siren. Frei details the racial, political, and sexual machinations of American Olympic officials and sets them against the grand maneuvering of the Nazi Party. Thoroughly researched, Frei's book reads like a true story and will have you convinced it all happened just this way.

Hillenbrand, Laura

Unbroken. A World War II Story of Survival, Resilience, and Redemption. 2010. Random House, ISBN 9781400064168. 496p.

Seabiscuit author Hillenbrand writes an epic biography of Louis Zamperini, a runner who competed in Hitler's Olympics, became part of the U.S. Air Force during World War II, and having been shot down over the ocean, was finally rescued by the Japanese ending up a POW. His story is remarkable, and Hillenbrand turns her many years of research into a gripping narrative that never falters. She not only interviewed Zamperini many times, but also family members and other POWs. One of 2010's most highly acclaimed books. ★

John, David

Flight from Berlin. 2012. Harper, ISBN 9780062091567. 372p.

John's debut novel is the story of Eleanor Emerson, an American swimmer, and Richard Denham, a British reporter, and is set at the Berlin Olympics. They have an unexpected love affair amid the politically charged games and readers are treated to a thrilling tale of suspense and international conspiracy. ★

Schaap, Jeremy

Triumph: The Untold Story of Jesse Owens and Hitler's Olympics. 2007. Houghton Mifflin Harcourt, ISBN 9780618688227. 288p.

One of the most famous athletes in the history of all sports, Jesse Owens's impact on the entire world at the 1936 Berlin games is impossible to overestimate. In winning four gold medals, he dispelled the myth of Aryan superiority that Hitler was so intent on proving. Schaap tells his story in thrilling detail using previously unavailable interviews and archives while adroitly carrying us step by step to the dramatic conclusion.

Walters, Guy

▶ *Berlin Games: How the Nazi's Stole the Olympic Dream.* 2007. Harper Perennial, ISBN 9780060874131. 400p.

Of all the books on this list that are specific to the 1936 Berlin Olympics, Walters gives us the most complete history of those monumental games. He not only analyzes the games themselves, but also sets the political context of the years before and after that eventful summer. The Nazi regime planned on using the Olympics to showcase their sporting supremacy and Walters shows how they convinced Western nations to compete even though many considered boycotting. For fans of sports, political and cultural history. ★

Sports amid Chaos

Even during the most trying times, athletes have continued to play scheduled games of sport. Maybe because we cling to what is considered normal or we need an escape from the everyday reality that keeps us awake through the night, we look forward to what we know to be a game. These books show us that other countries cope with chaos in much the same way.

Albone, Tim

Out of the Ashes: The Remarkable Rise and Rise of the Afghanistan Cricket Team. 2011. Virgin Books, ISBN 9780753522479. 304p.

This is the companion book to a 2010 documentary made by Tim Albone, a *Times* journalist working in Afghanistan, about the country's cricket team. When the team began playing in 2001, it was ranked 90th in the world. It has recently risen close to the top 10. The remarkable rise in the team's fortunes against all reasonable odds is due to Taj Malik, a refugee from the 1979 Soviet war. A true story of an underdog succeeding leaves us with a renewed sense of belief that almost anything is possible.

Ayub, Awista

Kabul Girls Soccer Club. 2009. Hyperion, ISBN 9781401310257. 246p.

Another look at war torn Afghanistan, this time from the perspective of eight girls brought to America in 2004 to play soccer. Author Ayub tells the stories of each of the girls who bring with them a unique experience growing up in Afghanistan under Taliban rule. What they all share is a love of soccer. We follow their lives as they arrive in the United States in 2004 to attend soccer camps around the country and see the differences in culture between the two countries, especially how it affects women.

Benaron, Naomi 🏆

▶ *Running the Rift: A Novel.* 2012. Algonquin Books, ISBN 9781616201944. 400p.

This debut novel from author Benaron was one of the most lauded books of 2012. It tells the tale of Jean Patrick Nkuba who believes he will someday represent his country at the Olympics and how he uses running to escape from the horror of his everyday life. Through his eyes, we experience the details of the Rwandan violence that was so prevalent at the beginning of the 1990s. A Bellwether prize winner. ★

Lomong, Lopez

Running for My Life: One Lost Boy's Journey from the Killing Fields of Sudan to the Olympic Games. 2012. Thomas Nelson, ISBN 9781595555151. 240p.
Ⓨ Ⓐ

An exceptional memoir of a Sudanese boy who is kidnapped during his country's civil war and against remarkable odds finds himself competing for the United States at the 2008 Olympic Games. Lomong's life is an inspiring tale of faith and talent that will appeal to runners as well as those interested in Sudanese history.

Powell, Robert Andrew

This Love Is Not for Cowards: Salvation and Soccer in Ciudad Juárez. 2012. Bloomsbury, ISBN 9781608197187. 272p.

To explore the connection between an athletic team and its fans is not a new story. But in a town where "murder is effectively legal" just across the U.S. border and the subject of immigration has become a focal point of American politics, this story seems like it was taken from today's headlines. In the best tradition of literary journalism, Powell follows the Indios, the town's hard-luck soccer team, as their status is threatened and violence is everywhere. ★

St. John, Warren

Outcasts United: The Story of a Refugee Soccer Team That Changed a Town. 2009. Spiegel and Grau, ISBN 9780385522038. 307p. [Y][A]

This is the stirring account of a refugee soccer team, the Fugees who are forced to resettle in a small American town. They have come from the Middle East, Africa, and the Balkans and their stories along with those of their Jordanian coach and the town itself combines to make this an inspiring read.

Winokur, W. William

■ *The Perfect Game.* 2008. Kissena Park Press, ISBN 9780976850816. 368p. [Y][A]

Monterrey, Mexico, 1957. A ragtag group of kids and a reluctant coach with only a dream to inspire them. That dream is to escape their slum surroundings and travel to the United States to play in the Little League World Series. Based on a true story, this novel is a delight to read.

Tools of the Trade—Equipment

Bats, balls, shoes, pucks, saddles. Every sport has its gear and its objects to hit, throw, swing, or kick. Here you will find books that talk about the iconic gear and origins of those oddly shaped things that are the center of our favorite sports.

Fox, John

The Ball: Discovering the Object of the Game. 2012. Harper Perennial, ISBN 9780061881794. 400p.

An insightful and meaningful exploration of the world of games with balls, Fox's book provides a splendid account into not just the games we play but why we play them and of what our ballgames tell us about ourselves. Well researched and written, it will appeal to anyone who likes a good narrative about an interesting subject.

Hample, Zack

The Baseball: Stunts, Scandals, and Secrets beneath the Stitches. 2011. Anchor Books, ISBN 9780307475459. 356p.

Here is the inside scoop on what's inside a baseball and how it has changed over the past 170 years. Author Hample is also quite the ball collector and he shares his secrets on how best to position yourself at ballparks to grab a foul ball. He also devotes chapters to balls as souvenirs, how to get a player to throw you a ball, and the top 10 stadiums for ball hawking. Will be enjoyed by anyone who loves a good game of catch.

Hoppel, Joe

▶ *Best by Number: Who Wore What with Distinction.* 2006. Sporting News, ISBN 9780892048489. 224p.

So have you noticed that wherever you go these days, a sporting event certainly, but even in restaurants or at a mall, there is someone wearing a jersey with a favorite player on it? Have you noticed what an industry it has become? Mostly popular are the major sports but not exclusively. This book is not really about the uniforms that players wear, but how popular the replica jerseys have become. Each number from 00 to 99 is discussed and one person is named the "King" of that number. Who is most associated with #32 or #44? Read the book and find out. Includes players' statistics and biographical information.

Magee, David and Philip Shirley

Sweet Spot: 125 Years of Baseball and Louisville Slugger. 2009. Triumph Books, ISBN 9781600781766. 176p.

Here's the story of how the most revered baseball bat came into existence and how it has dominated the market ever since. Ballplayers from Babe Ruth to Ted Williams to Derek Jeter would never consider using anything else.

McRae, Jim, Jim Hynes, and Gary Smith

Saving Face: The Art and History of the Goalie Mask. 2008. Wiley, ISBN 9780470155585. 160p.

During a game in 1959, Montreal Canadian goalie Jacques Plant was hit in the face by a hockey puck. To everyone's surprise, he soon emerged with a hockey mask, the first to do so, and impacted the game forever. This book consists of interviews with players and a photographic history that takes us through the evolution of the goalie mask.

Rovell, Darren

First in Thirst: How Gatorade Turned the Science of Sweat into a Cultural Phenomenon. 2005. AMACOM, ISBN 9780814410950. 256p.

Author Rovell chronicles every milestone of the company's history as Gatorade has dominated the sports drink market for over 40 years. With refreshing candor, *First in Thirst* also offers an inside look at the negotiations, lawsuits, product strategies, lucky breaks, and even the missteps (there have not been many) during Gatorade's reign. Certainly, this book will appeal to those interested in the business of sports, but it's also for those who watch athletes guzzle this stuff and wonder why it seems to be the only drink in town.

Skinner, Tina and Melissa Cardona
The Sneaker Book: 50 Years of Sports Shoe Design. 2007 (2005). Schiffer Publishing, ISBN 9780764321887. 256p.

Tennis shoes are called sneakers now I guess. Anyone remember Keds? Those were cool tennis shoes when I was a kid. I still buy tennis shoes rather than sneakers. (But enough about me.) This book covers a broad range of sneaker design over 50 years. We follow the evolution in styles and the changes in what tennis shoes have now come to represent. We learn about Nike and Adidas, and how the shoes have become status symbols bringing athletes millions of dollars to wear and promote them. Enhanced with magazine photos of shoe advertisements over the years, this book will appeal to those interested in the fashion side of sports.

At the Movies—Craig's Favorite Books to Film

We watch sports, we play sports, and the books written about particular athletes or grand events transfer particularly well to the silver screen. The number of books to film in the realm of sports is stunning and movies often receive greater acclaim than the original stories. Because there are so many films to choose from, we decided to offer a few of our favorite films; not all are award winners or classics, but we can't seem to resist watching them over and over again. Richard claims that I have very little taste in film and this list serves to either enforce that fact or surprise him. The following titles are some of my favorite sports movies that came from books. I will watch these any time they are available. I also love *Rocky*, *Bull Durham*, *Miracle*, and a host of others, but the aforementioned are original screenplays.

🎬 *For the Love of the Game.* **1999**
Shaara, Michael
For the Love of the Game. 1997 (1991). Ballantine Books, ISBN 9780345408921. 160p.

Billy Chapel is a successful major league pitcher in the twilight of his career, pitching for the last time in a season that doesn't matter. Readers follow Chapel as he reflects on his career and his life as the game he is pitching progresses. Kevin Costner portrays Chapel and Kelly Preston plays his love interest in an intimate and powerful film adaptation of the book. I'm clearly biased here, as I haven't found a Costner sports movie I didn't enjoy (I liked *Waterworld* too).

▄ *Friday Night Lights.* **2004**
Bissinger, Buzz
Friday Night Lights: A Town, a Team, and a Dream. 1990. Da Capo Press, ISBN 9780201196771. 357p.

A *New York Times* #1 best seller, this book captured the imagination of readers all over America, and the film and television series was just as successful. Follow the fates of not only the football players, but also all of the townspeople of Odessa, Texas, whose hopes and dreams ride on the success of the Perlman Panthers. Full of great sports action, interesting characters, and larger themes concerning class, race, and politics, this story is destined to become a classic of sports film. ★

▄ *Hurricane.* **1999**
Carter, Rubin "Hurricane"
Sixteenth Round: From Number One Contender to Number 45472. 1974 (2011). Chicago Review Press, ISBN 9781569765678. 368p.

Chaiton, Sam and Terry Swinton
Lazarus and the Hurricane: The Freeing of Rubin "Hurricane" Carter. 1991 (2000). St. Martin's Griffin, ISBN 9780312253974. 344p.

Denzel Washington earned a Golden Globe Award for his emotional and evocative portrayal of Rubin "Hurricane" Carter, a successful middleweight boxer who was wrongly imprisoned for 22 years. Carter's own memoir and the second book by two of the people who worked on his defense team serve as the basis for the film. Carter's book is powerful and intimate, while *Lazarus* . . . shows the conviction and dedication of those that sought to help him.

▄ *Invictus.* **2009**
Carlin, John
Playing the Enemy: Nelson Mandela and the Game That Made a Nation. 2009. Penguin Press, ISBN 9781594201745. 274p.

Mandela, South Africa's president in the first free election in 1994, decided that the best way to unite all people in his country together was through their rugby team, the Springboks. This true story is brought to screen in realistic fashion and the South African people shine as they rally around the commonality of rugby. Morgan Freeman plays President Mandela and Matt Damon plays the Springbok's captain Francois Pienaar, in this uplifting story of faith and pride through sports. ★

▄ *The Legend of Bagger Vance.* **2001**
Pressfield, Steven
The Legend of Bagger Vance: A Novel of Golf and the Game of Life. 1996 (1995). Avon Books/Spike, ISBN 9780688140489. 272p.

Fictional golfer Rannulph Junah battles his memories of the Great War while trying to rekindle his golf prowess and represent his town in a grand golf match with actual historical champions Bobby Jones and Walter Hagen. Along comes a mysterious stranger who offers to caddy for Junah and straighten out his game and his state of mind. Magical realism at its best, the movie stars Matt Damon and Will Smith in this thoroughly entertaining film.

Million Dollar Baby. 2004
Toole, F. X.
Million Dollar Baby: Stories from the Corner. 2005 (2000). HarperCollins, ISBN 9780060198206. 256p.

    This movie won five Academy Awards in 2005, including best picture. Clint Eastwood directs and stars in this adaptation of a short story about a crusty old boxing trainer and a young woman who just wants a chance to fight. The author of the story, Toole, was in the fight game as a manager and a cutman for much of his life, and a most remarkable sidebar is that he was 70 years old when he published this title—his first collection of stories that was originally published in 2000 as *Rope Burns: Stories from the Corner*.

Semi-Tough. 1977
Jenkins, Dan
Semi-Tough: A Novel. 2006 (1973). Da Capo Press, ISBN 9781560258599. 318p.

    Today's NFL players can't hold a candle to Billy Clyde Puckett (Burt Reynolds) and Marvin "Shake" Tiller (Chris Kristofferson). The book is a classic that *Sports Illustrated* puts in its top 100 of all time, and this first-person account of the antics of pro running back Puckett and his company of cohorts reads like a swingers account of the NFL in the 1970s, but the book does have its thoughtful moments as Puckett and Shake try to figure out their lives after football. The movie doesn't convey Jenkins great tone and style, so it is better to read the book first.

At the Movies 2—Richard's Favorite Books to Film

    These are some of my favorite films based on books. Not all are great movies, but most are worth a watch. Once again baseball movies tend to dominate the genre, but I've tried to bring a wide variety of sports to the list. From horses to heartbreak and humor to romance, these movies will bring out a range of emotions. Craig thinks I'm kind of a movie snob, but I'm not sure he even realizes that movies used to be predominantly black and white.

The Bingo Long Traveling All-Stars & Motor Kings. 1976
Brashler, William
The Bingo Long Traveling All-Stars & Motor Kings. 1993 (1973). University of Illinois Press, ISBN 9780252062872. 280p.

This sometimes hilarious film is loosely based on Brashler's novel and stars Billy Dee Williams, James Earl Jones, and Richard Pryor. It's set in the segregated south in 1939 and is about a pitcher who tired of getting bossed around by the less than ethical managers of the Negro leagues decides to form his own barnstorming team. The team flourishes and along the way captures the hearts of many fans. A fine script and crisp direction make this a worthy watch. The cast can't be beat either.

The Black Stallion. **1979**
Farley, Walter
The Black Stallion. 1991 (1941). Random House, ISBN 9780679813439. 187p.

What I remember most about this film based on the classic novel from 1941 is its gorgeous cinematography and how the first half of the film is almost pure visual cinema. The story is a classic one as boy and stallion are the only survivors of a sinking ship and the bond they forge culminates in a classic horse race. A true family film that can be savored many times.

Eight Men Out. **1988**
Asinof, Eliot
▶ *Eight Men Out: The Black Sox and the 1919 World Series.* 2000 (1963). Holt, ISBN 9780805065374. 336p.

Director/writer John Sayles and a stellar cast do themselves proud in this adaptation of Asinof's classic novel. The story revolves around eight players on the Chicago White Sox, some of who decided to intentionally lose games in the World Series because of their disgruntlement with the meager salaries they received from skinflint owner Charles Comiskey. Each of them has a fascinating story. Starring John Cusack, Charlie Sheen, and D. B. Sweeney as clueless Joe Jackson. I watched this again recently and it was as compelling as ever.

The Express. **2008**
Gallagher, Robert
Ernie Davis: The Elmira Express. 2008 (1999). Bartleby Pr., ISBN 9780910155755. 190p.

A drama based on the life of college football hero Ernie Davis, the first African American to win the Heisman Trophy. Davis followed the great Jim Brown at Syracuse University and faced much of the same discrimination Brown did. He couldn't even attend his own banquet dinner because the venue didn't serve blacks. Then, having been drafted by the Cleveland Browns to be paired with Brown at running back, Davis was diagnosed with leukemia and never played a single down in the pros. I vividly remember this drama as it played out in real time. The film paints a realistic picture of Davis's relationship with his coach at Syracuse (played by Dennis Quaid) and is mostly faithful to the source material. Not quite the tearjerker of *Brian's Song* but heartbreaking nonetheless.

■ *The Harder They Fall.* **1956**
Schulberg, Budd
  The Harder They Fall. 2007 (1947). Ivan R. Dee, ISBN 9781566631075. 357p.
    Humphrey Bogart plays Eddie Willis, an unemployed newspaperman who gets caught up in a boxing scandal in this his final film. Rod Steiger also stars as a corrupt fight manager and they both shine in this black and white classic.

■ *The Hustler.* **1961**
Tevis, Walter
  The Hustler. 2002 (1959). Thunder's Mouth Press, ISBN 9781560254737. 224p.
    As *The Hustler*'s "Fast" Eddie Felson, Paul Newman created a classic antihero, charismatic but fundamentally flawed, and nobody's role model. Felson, one of the great pool players of all time, didn't just want to beat you, he wanted to humiliate you. And this flaw was part of his undoing. Focusing on his classic match against Minnesota Fats (Jackie Gleason), the movie was filmed in glistening black and white. Also starring George C. Scott and Piper Laurie, the film is a simmering classic. ★

■ *Seabiscuit.* **2008**
Hillenbrand, Laura
  Seabiscuit: An American Legend. 2001. Random House, ISBN 9780375502912. 399p.
    A widely acclaimed movie based on a great best-selling book about a magnificent horse. It is a classic underdog story with Seabiscuit morphing into the champion we have come to love due to the care of his owner, trainer, and jockey. The film does a fine job mixing action and emotion while remaining faithful to its source material. To be enjoyed with the whole family. ★

■ *Tall Story.* **1960**
Nemerov, Howard
  The Homecoming Game. 1992 (1957). University of Missouri Press, ISBN 9780826208705. 264p.
    This is probably the only real guilty pleasure on my list. Kind of a sappy romance spliced with some college basketball action, the film stars Anthony Perkins and a young Jane Fonda in her debut film. Also look for Robert Redford in an uncredited role as a teammate of Perkins. I remember seeing this on TV and most often couldn't resist watching again. Not well-received upon its release, the movie holds up surprisingly well as a relic from a more innocent time.

Chapter Four

Language

Form and the writing arts are the focus of this section, and while sports may not be a hotbed of literary excellence, the writers who bring the game to life on the page have a rare gift for expressing emotional events and spectacular settings. The diary, poetry, interviews, and humor, as well as novelists who use the game as a stage for thought-provoking themes provide a view of sport sometimes more vivid and fulfilling than the events themselves.

The Art of the Essay and Article

How much does sports play a part in the fabric of America? Just look at the variety of professional sports writers, authors, and others who offer concise, lyrical, and sometimes brash opinions of sports. Baseball reigns supreme here; maybe it's due to the long history of the game compared to other American sports, or maybe there is just a surplus amount of time to ruminate during the game. However, we have gathered some outstanding compilations from writers past and present.

Angell, Roger
   The Summer Game. 1972. Viking, ISBN 9780670681648. 303p.
       Angell, fiction editor of *The New Yorker*, presents a series of essays on baseball as it was in the 1960s and early 1970s. Delightful and poignant, these stories describe the game as it was changing: indoor fields, The Expos, California baseball, and, as a New York writer, the demise and triumphs of New York baseball. ★

Berkow, Ira
The Minority QB and Other Lives in Sports. 2002. Ivan R. Dee, ISBN 9781566634229. 320p.

> Berkow is a Pulitzer-winning journalist from the *New York Times* and here he gathers his sports articles on a variety of themes from superstars to little league to everything in between. A fine stylistic writer, Berkow captures details that transcend the sport and he often delves into details outside of the game.

Feinstein, John
▶ *One on One: Behind the Scenes with the Greats in the Game.* 2011. Little, Brown and Co., ISBN 9780316079044. 533p.

> Follow Feinstein as he revisits some of his most memorable sports stories and interviews of his life. From his early days with Bobby Knight to interviews with Tiger Woods, John McEnroe, and others, Feinstein weaves a concise narrative of great people and grand events.

Halberstam, David
Everything They Had: Sports Writing from David Halberstam. 2008. Hyperion, ISBN 9781401309909. 401p.

> Winner of the Pulitzer prize for his writings in Vietnam, Halberstam wrote with passion and clarity about sports of all kinds. This volume presents a cross section of his writing from his early days at his college paper to later articles for the *New York Times*, ESPN.com, and many others. Beautiful and intimate stories from a legendary sports writer.

Jordan, Pat
The Best Sports Writing of Pat Jordan. 2008. Persea, ISBN 9780892553396. 400p.

> Few writers can bring out the authenticity in their subjects like Pat Jordan. He has written for *GQ*, *Sports Illustrated*, and a host of other sources, and his unique ability to let the story tell itself through his stylistic writing provides for entertaining and enlightening reading. Here he compiles some of his best stories on a host of athletes including Roger Clemens, The William Sisters, and even Sylvester Stallone. ★

Liebling, A. J.
The Sweet Science and Other Writings. 2009. Library of America, ISBN 9781598530407. 1,057p.

> Originally published in 1966 and hailed by *Sports Illustrated* as one of the best sports books of all time, this collection presents Liebling's writing on boxing greats such as Sugar Ray Robinson and Rocky Marciano. Liebling brings the world of boxing to life with elegant prose, lush descriptions, and artful honesty. ★

MacGregor, Roy
Wayne Gretzky's Ghost: And Other Tales from a Lifetime in Hockey. 2011. Random House Canada, ISBN 9780307357410. 400p.

MacGregor is considered one of the greatest hockey writers today and he has drawn acclaim for his other fiction and nonfiction work as well. Here he selects some of his best columns arranged into sections such as Legends of the Game, Stars, Bar Debates, and Anguish, to name a few. The title story relates MacGregor's time as a ghostwriter for the "Great One."

Smith, Red and Daniel Okrent, editor.

American Pastimes: The Very Best of Red Smith. 2013. Library of America, ISBN 9781598532173. 480p.

This outstanding *Library of America* publication brings to the forefront one of the greats of all time. Red Smith was the first sportswriter to win the Pulitzer prize for commentary (1976), and he created the blueprint for successful sports reporting that other writers on this list have tried to follow (Berkow wrote a Red Smith biography in 1986). A great collection of American stories from the man who (may) have been the first to say "Writing is easy. You just open a vein and bleed."

Will, George

Bunts: Curt Flood, Camden Yards, Pete Rose, and Other Reflections on Baseball. 1998. Scribner, ISBN 9780684838205. 352p.

Will takes his writing talents to the diamonds in this collection of baseball articles ranging from 1974 to 1997. Will's art with language shines as he relates tales of his own subpar baseball skills, his long-suffering life as a Cubs Fan, and stories of great players and others involved in America's pastime.

These Guys Are Funny—Humor in Sports

Comedy and sports go hand in hand, whether highlight reels of bumbling plays or simple the fun of camaraderie, soul searching, and competition. This category contains a cross section of the best and, sometimes, accidental humorists in the game.

Culpepper, Chuck

Bloody Confused! A Clueless American Sportswriter Seeks Solace in English Soccer. 2008. Broadway Books, ISBN 9780767928083. 250p.

Disillusioned with American sports and its narcissistic athletes, steroid controversies, and labor strikes, *Los Angeles Times* reporter Culpepper takes to the pitch and immerses himself in English Premier League Soccer. He provides an entertaining primer on the sport, and while learning the intricacies of the game and the passion of its fans, he finds a new team to call his own: The Portsmouth Football Club. ★

Hiaasen, Carl

The Downhill Lie: A Hacker's Return to a Ruinous Sport. 2009 (2008). Vintage, ISBN 9780307280459. 224p.

After a 32-layoff, a middle-aged slightly unhealthy writer decides to try his hand at golf again. Good for readers but not so good for Hiaasen, who was not a very good golfer when he was younger. He reminisces about his father and golf and then moves into daily adventures with friends, other writers, and golf professionals as he tries to improve his game. Hiaasen's self-deprecating humor and conversational tone is delightful and entertaining.

Krewson, John and Mike DiCenzo
▶ *The Ecstasy of Defeat: Sports Reporting at Its Finest by the Editors of the Onion.* 2011. Hyperion, ISBN 9781401310721. 272p.

From the forward written by "Anabolic Steroids" and how it saved sports reporting, *The Onion* staff pulls no punches as it pokes fun at athletes, teams, cities, and just about everyone involved in sports. The tabloid style format is entertaining, easy to read, and includes photographs and captions. Irreverent, gut-busting funny, and at times candid and truthful, this one will bring tears to your eyes.

McLennan, Jamie and Ian Mendes
The Best Seat in the House: Stories from the NHL—Inside the Room, On the Ice and On the Bench. 2012. Wiley, ISBN 9781118302538. 256p.

An NHL goalie for 17 years, McLennan is affectionately known as "Noodles" in the hockey world. He played for five different NHL teams and has the stories to prove it. From rookie hazing to unfortunate incidents on and off the ice, this current *NHL Network* analyst and journalist describes his unique career as a backup goalie. From running over an opposing team's mascot to hiding a hot dog in his glove because he wanted a snack, McLennan's stories will leave readers in stitches.

Reilly, Rick
Hate Mail from Cheerleaders: And Other Adventures from the Life of Rick Reilly. Sports Illustrated, ISBN 9781933821122. 320p.

Many a subscriber to *Sports Illustrated* opens a new issue directly to the back page to read "The Life of Reilly." Not all of these articles are humorous in nature, but enough of them are to merit placing it in this category. Reilly selects 100 of his best columns and his subjects range from professional athletes to, um, cheerleaders. Note to self: "Do not ever say that cheerleading is not a sport." ★

Simmons, Russell
The Book of Basketball: The NBA According to the Sports Guy. 2009. ESPN, ISBN 9780345520104. 752p.

The irreverent and humorous "Sports Guy "from ESPN presents his take on great players and the game in general. Simmons breaks down MVPs, rates the best players, and offers some hilarious "what-if" scenarios sure to entertain fans and spark a few debates. Even the footnotes are funny in this behemoth of a book as Simmons argues, sometimes with himself, about how the legends and contemporaries stack up in the NBA. ★

St. Amant, Mark
Just Kick It: Tales of an Underdog, Overage, Out-of-Place Semi-Pro Football Player. 2006. Scribner, ISBN 9780743286756. 256p.

Fantasy football writer and mediocre high school soccer player decides to find the glory of the game by becoming the kicker for The Boston Panthers, a semipro football team. An authentic fish out of water tale, he finds himself immersed in the positive forces of the team mentality and he writes about his adventures and his fellow teammates with humor, friendship, and respect. ★

Thompson, Hunter S.
Hey Rube: Blood Sport, the Bush Doctrine, and the Downward Spiral of Dumbness. 2004. Simon and Schuster, ISBN 9780684873190. 246p.

Hunter Thompson (1937–2005) of *Fear and Loathing in Las Vegas* collects memorable columns from his ESPN.com writings. Not for the faint of heart, Hunter takes aim at the state of sports and athletes while simultaneously commenting on politics and life in America. His columns range from rants on presidential politics to the thinning of the talent pool in the NFL, from the NBA to the Kentucky Derby, and no one is safe from his wrath. Not so subtle, but very enjoyable.

Titus, Mark
Don't Put Me in Coach: My Incredible NCAA Journey from the End of the Bench to the End of the Bench. 2012. Doubleday, ISBN 9780385535106. 272p.

Here's a word that should be used more and is an apt description of Titus's book: shenanigans. A walk-on basketball player for The Ohio State University, he logged nine points in his college career. He takes readers on a hilarious jaunt through his basketball career and all of the pranks, fun, and lapses in judgment along the way. A bit enthusiastic with the potty humor and college hijinks, Titus will have you laughing out loud if you go for that sort of thing.

Behind the Pen (Keyboard)—Writers' Lives

This category consists of sports writers writing about their lives and in doing so let us in on what many consider a privileged lifestyle. They get to hang out with our heroes and most of them seem to understand that. We also feature some fiction that spotlights another side of writers' lives that aren't so glamorous but much more human.

Berkow, Ira

Full Swing. 2006. Ivan R. Dee, ISBN 9781566637558. 304p.

Berkow's memoir is a must read as he relives his upbringing in Chicago and his slow rise to *New York Times* columnist. Great celebrity bits are included with Muhammad Ali, Willie Mays, and a few nonsports personalities. Another distinguished writer that just happened to make a career of sports writing. Because Berkow has written about more than sports during his career, this memoir may appeal to some nonsports fans.

Brennan, Christine

Best Seat in the House: A Father, a Daughter, a Journey through Sports. 2006. Scribner, ISBN 9780743254366. 304p.

Brennan is probably the best known and most widely read sports columnist in the United States. Her career began in 1981 with the *Miami Herald* and she has been covering premier sporting events ever since. Her father told her at an early age to dream big, that she could do anything she wanted, and she certainly followed his advice. Filled with anecdotes including interviewing naked players in the locker room, her book is heartfelt, touching, and instructive.

Dawidoff, Nicholas

The Crowd Sounds Happy: A Story of Love, Madness, and Baseball. 2009 (2008). Vintage ISBN 9780375700071. 288p.

You might remember Dawidoff as the editor of *Baseball: A Literary Anthology* from a previous category. Here, he turns his attention inward as he looks back on growing up in the 1970s and on the fractured family life that shaped his childhood. With exquisite prose, Dawidoff reflects on growing up in the East, his passion for the Red Sox, and the education that brought the success as a writer that is so obviously on display here.

Deford, Frank

▶ *Over Time: My Life as a Sportswriter.* 2013 (2012). Grove Press, ISBN 9780802146069. 368p.

A stalwart of American sports writing, Deford has just about seen and covered it all since he began writing for *Sports Illustrated* in 1962. He has also written novels, won numerous awards, and continues to provide commentary for National Public Radio. His memoir is entertaining and exceedingly witty to boot. He pays tribute to writers who came before him and athletes who have thrilled him. ★

Ford, Richard

The Sportswriter. 1995 (1986). Vintage, ISBN 9780679762102. 375p.

The first book in Ford's Bascombe Trilogy, *The Sportswriter* introduces us to Frank Bascombe, an average middle-aged man. Things have not been going so well for Frank: his son has died and his wife has just divorced him. The story is moody and at times depressing and destroys the glamorous mystique of sports writing. The sequel to this novel *Independence Day* won the Pulitzer prize for fiction in 1996. ★

Kahn, Roger
The Boys of Summer. 2006 (1971). Harper Perennial, ISBN 9780060883966. 512p.
> A glorious work that some believe to be the greatest of all written on baseball. It could fit in many places in this book: In "Setting" as a nonpareil description of the city of Brooklyn throughout the 1930s–1950s, in "Mood" as a nostalgic look back at a more innocent time, and again in "Language" for those interested in works that go beyond sports. It is a memoir of a young sports reporter covering his favorite team, and later as an older man interviewing the heroes of his youth one last time. For a more thorough memoir, see Kahn's *Into My Own: The Remarkable People and Events That Shaped a Life* (2007). ★

Karunatilaka, Shehan
The Legend of Pradeep Mathew: A Novel. 2011. Graywolf Press, ISBN 9781555976118. 397p.
> An aging sportswriter's liver is pretty much shot due to heavy drinking throughout his life. While researching a documentary on the best cricket players from Sri Lanka, he undertakes a search for missing cricket player and once famous Pradeep Mathew. Along the way, he learns more than he bargained for. An amusing and touching rumination on a sport the author obviously loves and a unique portrayal of life in Sri Lanka.

Wojciechowski, Gene
About 80 Percent Luck: A Sportswriter's Tale. 2001. Total Sports, ISBN 9781930844087. 292p.
> Wojciechowski is a senior national sports columnist for ESPN, so he brings a wealth of inside information to this novel. Chicago sportswriter Joe Riley has seen better days. He drinks too much and his career seems to be slipping away. When told to head out to Arizona for exhibition baseball season, he accepts the assignment and slowly begins to turn things around. A light read with lots of humor, the book goes down like a beer at a baseball game.

Nonsports Writers Writing about Sports

Here are some books by eminent writers who decided to delve into writing about sports if only for a short time. Many of them are beloved for their other works, but their fans will follow them anywhere.

Casey, John
Room for Improvement: Notes on a Dozen Lifelong Sports. 2011. Alfred A. Knopf, ISBN 9780307700025. 231p.

Casey has been a devoted and passionate outdoor sportsman throughout his life and in this book, he recounts, via essay, some of his most interesting experiences. He writes about his experiences with judo, cross-country skiing, and marathoning. As an award-winning novelist, Casey writes with grace and wit, and his writing will appeal to lovers of language as well as the adventurous sportsman in us all.

Foer, Franklin and Marc Tracy, editors.
Jewish Jocks: An Unorthodox Hall of Fame. 2012. Twelve, ISBN 9781455516131. 304p.

While a few of these 50 or so short essays are by sports writers, most are by writers who ordinarily don't write about sports. All the writers find a way to tie their portraits to religion in some way. And of course all the writers and subjects are Jewish. From Sandy Koufax to Marc Spitz to Arnold Rothstein (gambler who instigated the 1919 Black Sox scandal), all essays are thoughtful and well written.

Goodwin, Doris Kearns
▶ *Wait Till Next Year: A Memoir.* 1997. Scribner, ISBN 9780684824895. 272p.

Historian Goodwin hits a grand slam here with her memoir of growing up a Brooklyn Dodgers fan and how the bond that developed with her father and their mutual love of the game has impacted her life. She deftly recounts games, players, and most dramatically the Dodgers move to Los Angeles. She brings a historian's perspective and a deep and abiding enthusiasm for baseball to her writing, and we share her losses of family and triumphs in her career.

Murakami, Haruki
What I Talk About When I Talk About Running. 2009 (2008). Vintage, ISBN 9780307389831. 192p.

Japanese author Murakami has been a long-distance runner since the early 1980s. Novel writing and marathoning are two extremely solitary undertakings and Marakami seeks to combine both in this memoir. The book will appeal to runners who are looking for more than a how-to set of instructions. The author delves into the reasons why running is so appealing and rewarding, and his musings will surely have runners nodding their heads in agreement. While some of the book is presented in diary form, most is a narrative that is part travelogue, part self-help, and includes useful tips for runners.

Oates, Joyce Carol
On Boxing (P.S.). 2006 (1987). Harper Perennial Modern Classics, ISBN 9780060874506. 304p.

Novelist Oates explains: "No one whose interest began as mine did in childhood—as an offshoot of my father's interest is likely to think of boxing as something else, a metaphor . . . Life is like boxing, in many respects. But boxing is only like boxing." Oates explores much more than boxing in these essays. She relates boxing to the art and sexuality of the day and gets to the heart of its appeal for so many of us. For those fans more in tune with the poetry of the sport.

O'Neill, Molly
  Mostly True: A Memoir of Family, Food, and Baseball. 2008. Scribner, ISBN 9780743232692. 288p.

  O'Neill is a celebrated writer and food critic, and this memoir of her life growing up in Columbus is certainly captivating. The first of six siblings and the only girl, she watched as her brothers all forayed into Little League Baseball and one, Paul, eventually became a star outfielder with the New York Yankees. But the book is not about them; it is about Molly's life and where it has taken her. A refreshing read, it goes down like a good soufflé.

Updike, John
  Hub Fans Bid Kid Adieu: John Updike on Ted Williams. 2010 (1977). Library of America Edition, ISBN 9781598530711. 47p.

  This essay was originally published in *The New Yorker* magazine in the aftermath of Ted Williams's final game in 1960. Iconic author Updike was at Fenway Park that day like many others to pay tribute to one of the greatest hitters the game has ever seen. Not surprisingly, his final at bat produced a home run. This 60th anniversary commemorative edition was prepared with Updike's assistance just months before his death.

Wodehouse, P. G.
  The Golf Omnibus. 1973. Simon and Schuster, ISBN 9780671216184. 467p.

  This entertaining, stimulating, and vibrant work from the inimitable Wodehouse will leave you laughing and feeling pretty good about your golf game too. His characters are obsessed with golf, but we don't need to be golfers to appreciate the humor or the obsessions. Many believe the use of language here is unsurpassed and after reading these stories one would be hard pressed to disagree. A true classic. ★

For Literary Enthusiasts—Sports and So Much More

Nonsports writers also wrote the books on this list, but they are not always as obvious about sports in particular, more often using them to frame a much different story. Five of them are novels, and the category also includes one play and an essay. Some tackle larger issues, while others are purely about a particular game or event. All have in common a love of language and a masterful talent for telling a story.

Fountain, Ben 🏆
  Billy Lynn's Long Halftime Walk. 2012. Ecco, ISBN 9780060885595. 320p.

  One of the most highly acclaimed novels of 2012 has very little to do with sports except that it takes place at a Dallas Cowboys football game on Thanksgiving day. Billy Lynn and his Bravo squad mates are here to be honored for a firefight that took place against Iraqi insurgents, and this is part of a bizarre victory tour they are on. As the day wears on, Fountain manages to comment on many of the social and political issues of the time. ★

Harbach, Chad
The Art of Fielding. 2012 (2011). Back Bay Books, ISBN 9780316126670. 544p.
 Harbach's debut novel is an entertaining amalgam of American life centered on small-town college baseball. It isn't really about baseball, but the characters are involved with the game and much of it is set on or near a baseball field. There is romance, deception, and bad behavior; and on the periphery, there is an overachieving underdog college team. It revolves around a player who suddenly loses the talent he has been developing his whole life, but maybe he gains something much more important. It will disappoint those looking for strictly a baseball story but reward those who don't mind an unexpected plot twist or two. ★

Quick, Matthew
Silver Linings Playbook. 2012 (2008). Sarah Crichton Books, ISBN 9780374533571. 304p.
 This debut novel about a down-on-his-luck former history teacher was made into an Oscar-nominated film in 2012, and was one of the most popular movies of the year. A lifelong fan of the Philadelphia Eagles, protagonist Pat Peoples has just been released from a mental institution into the custody of his mother. His delusions include hopes to reconcile with his estranged wife. What follows are sometimes comic and other times heartbreaking as Pat tries to put his life back together. Dysfunctional only begins to describe his family, but Quick's offbeat story is a real crowd-pleaser.

Roth, Philip
The Great American Novel. 1995 (1973). Vintage, ISBN 9780679749066. 416p.
 A baseball novel unlike any other with a plot so convoluted that any attempt at description would be of no help whatsoever. Suffice to say, this is Roth's love letter to baseball, full of satire on religion, politics, and sex. For Roth devotees, literature lovers, baseball fanatics, and those who appreciate great wit and humor, this is a book that you will turn to again and again. ★

Shapton, Leanne ♔
Swimming Studies. 2012. Blue Rider Press, ISBN 9780399158179. 336p.
 While she never made it to the Olympics, Shapton competed in the Canadian Olympic trials in 1988 and 1992. An artist and graphic novelist, she includes beautiful watercolor prints alongside her spare but emotional prose, revealing her life under water. Anyone who ever swam competitively will be duly impressed as it elegantly captures what it takes to compete. Winner of the 2012 National Book Critics Circle Award for Autobiography. ★

Wilson, August
Fences. 1986. Plume, ISBN 9780452264014. 101p.
  Wilson's play mixes comedy and drama as it explores the radical changes taking place in the second half of the century. Lead character Troy Maxson was a fine baseball player in his youth, but since there was yet to be professional black ballplayers, he was unable to pursue his dream. Now his son would like to play football and Troy is reluctant to let him. Winner of the Tony Award for Best Play when it premiered on Broadway in 1987, this two-act play is challenging yet rewarding for those who appreciate fine theater.

Winegardner, Mark
▶ *Crooked River Burning*. 2001. Mariner Books, ISBN 9780156014229. 592p.
  Only peripherally about the futility of the Cleveland Indians after 1954, this epic novel also charts the decline of a once proud city to national joke, no more fittingly symbolized than by the Cuyahoga River catching fire in 1969. Mixing fictional characters along with historical figures like Bill Veeck and Carl Stokes, Winegardner evokes a vivid slice of social history. ★

Historical Novels of the Game

  We come back to baseball as the most popular subject for historical fiction in sports. But we kept hunting and found some highly readable historical fiction ranging from the 1936 Olympics to Regency England boxing. Frank Deford's *Everybody's All-American* has the most general appeal; the story of a blue-chip quarterback's struggle with life after football is written with graceful prose and the vivid background of 1950s North Carolina. Sport themes in historical fiction may not be abundant, but these titles should pique the interest of fans of earlier times.

Deford, Frank
▶ ▣ *Everybody's All-American*. 2004 (1981). Da Capo Press, ISBN 9780306813757. 366p.
  Deford's classic novel examines college football, social mores in the 1950s south, and themes of loss and growth as we follow the extraordinary football career of North Carolina star Gavin Grey. The characters are king in this lively story, and the narration by Gray's young nephew is smart and compelling. Made into a popular movie starring Dennis Quaid, Jessica Lange, and Timothy Hutton, Hollywood changed the team to the LSU Tigers. ★

John, David
Flight from Berlin. 2012. Harper, ISBN 9780062091567. 372p.
  John's debut novel tells the story of American swimmer Eleanor Emerson and British reporter Richard Denham and is set at the 1936 Berlin Olympics. They have an unexpected love affair amid the politically charged

games and readers are treated to a thrilling tale of suspense and international conspiracy. ★

Fraser, George Macdonald
Black Ajax. 1999 (1998). Carroll and Graf, ISBN 978786706181. 256p.

Based on the true story of slave, boxer, and gentleman Tom Molineux, Frazier takes us vividly into the violent days of bare-knuckle boxing. Molineux won his freedom with his pugilistic prowess and lives in England enjoying a life of society. Frazier's use of multiple narrators and authentic dialect places readers squarely in Regency England. Can Molineux become champion or will his excesses and those against him win out?

King, Kevin
All of the Stars Came Out That Night. 2007 (2005). Plume Books, ISBN 9780525949053. 415p.

It's hard to describe the ambitious plot and sheer volume of historical characters in this outlandish story of a depression era all-star game between the best of white players versus the best of the Negro leagues. Add to the mix a pair of ambitious but bumbling criminals. Clarence Darrow, Walter Winchell, Satchel Paige, Joe DiMaggio, Shoeless Joe . . . this novel is a wondrous romp through 1930s history. ★

Levy, Burt
The Last Open Road: A Novel. 1994 (1998). Think Fast Ink, ISBN 9780964210721. 354p.

Few remember the glory days of open-road racing, but Levy recreates the excitement and lure of a time when some local mechanics could simply work on a car and get driving. Set in 1952, this humorous coming-of-age tale follows young grease monkey Buddy Palumbo as he embarks on an adventure of a lifetime.

Schilling, Peter
The End of Baseball. 2010 (2008). Ivan R. Dee, ISBN 9781566638487. 352p.

What if Bill Veeck had been able to buy a major league franchise and populate it with an entire team of Negro league players? Schilling creates a fascinating alternate history of a 1944 season that might have been. Including Negro league legends Satchel Paige and Josh Gibson, Veeck outfits the Philadelphia A's to be a winner. Fast-paced, witty, and original, Veeck's real-life antics and revolutionary ideas are amplified in this wholly enjoyable novel.

Wallace, Joseph
Diamond Ruby. 2010. Touchstone, ISBN 9781439160053. 464p.

In 1923 New York, young Ruby Lee Thomas is trying to find a way to support her nieces who are left in her care. Turns out, she can throw quite a fastball. Thomas's character is based on Jackie Mitchell, the first woman admitted to the

Negro leagues; she struck out Babe Ruth and so does Diamond Ruby. Wallace writes with strong historical detail, lush prose, and strong female characters to create a compelling novel.

The Fantastic—Novels That Stretch the Imagination

There is not an overabundance of literary novelists who take on sports as a subject; or if they do, it tends to be written for a young adult audience. Here we attempt to select some of the best and most recognizable authors who can turn a phrase, express a theme, and create a bit of wonder in their plots. It's no wonder that many of the titles listed have been adapted to film. Anthropomorphism, magical realism, a dash of the faerie, and a bit of the absurd make up this category so suspend belief, sit back, and enjoy.

Brock, Daryl
If I Never Get Back. 2007 (1989). Frog Books, ISBN 9781583941874. 432p.

Brock's debut novel is a doozy. It quickly begins with Sam Fowler, a discontented journalist whose family life has disintegrated, stepping off an Amtrak train and back into 1869. Here he becomes involved with the first great professional baseball team, the Cincinnati Red Stockings. Chocked full of period detail and perceptive insight into the early years of our national pastime, it is a book many return to every spring to whet their appetite for the coming baseball season.

Chabon, Michael
Summerland. 2011 (2002). Disney Hyperion, ISBN 9781423139959. 512p. [Y][A]

Follow 11-year-old Ethan Feld as he is transported to strange worlds by a mysterious baseball scout named Mr. Chiron "Ringfinger" Brown. The game is much more serious in the world of the ferishers, giants, and other creatures. It has implications that involve the survival of all of the worlds and even the well-being of Ethan's father. Chabon combines myth, legend, and folklore and spins a wonderful baseball yarn. While marketed as a YA novel, this title will appeal to fans of all ages.

Groom, Winston
🎬 *Forrest Gump.* 2012 (1986). Vintage Books, ISBN 9780307947390. 240p.

While strictly speaking this is not a sports novel, Forrest does excel at football, wrestling, ping-pong, and chess. The most fascinating thing about this novel is how much it differs from the popular film starring Tom Hanks. It's a bit more explicit, a shade darker at times, and uproariously funny. If the film were made more exacting, it would be *Forrest Gump: The Unrated Version.*

Kinsella, Joe ♔
▶ 🎬 *Shoeless Joe.* 1999 (1982). Mariner Books, ISBN 9780395957738. 272p.
"If you build it, he will come." This quote is repeated by a strange voice
that Ray Kinsella hears in his head and compels him to build a baseball field
in the middle of his Iowa cornfield. Immortalized by Kevin Costner on the
silver screen, this novel explores fathers, sons, creation versus destruction, and
family trust. As long-dead players begin to play baseball on Kinsella's field,
readers are treated to wonderful characters, vivid descriptions, and insightful
themes that are more nuanced than the film version. This novel won the 1982
Canada First Novel Award. ★

Malamud, Bernard
🎬 *The Natural.* 2003 (1952). Farrar, Straus and Giroux, ISBN 9780374502003. 231p.
Roy Hobbs has a gift and that gift is playing baseball. Readers are given a
front row seat as Hobbs is sidelined by an injury and reappears 15 years after his
initial try at becoming a big leaguer. In a story that is laced with myth and sym-
bolism, *The Natural* follows Hobbs and his Excalibur-like bat "Wonderboy" as
he navigates not only baseball, but also love, desire, and his quest for greatness.
The movie is entertaining, but the original story is much better. ★

Murphy, Michael
🎬 *Golf in the Kingdom.* 2011 (1972). Penguin Books, ISBN 9780143120902. 223p.
Set in 1956, a philosophy student on his way to study in India makes time
for a round of golf at Burningbush golf links in Scotland. There he meets Shivas
Irons, a golf professional and mystic; and Irons takes Murphy on a journey of
self-examination and reflection through golf. Widely praised as one of the best
golf novels of all time, Murphy's intimate first-person account and his attempt
to explain and analyze this fictional adventure make for a unique and enlightening read. ★

Plimpton, George
The Curious Case of Sidd Finch. 2004 (1987). Da Capo Press, ISBN
9781568582962. 296p. [Y][A]
This entry is an indulgence because the novel didn't receive great reviews.
The backstory is the best part: In 1985, George Plimpton published an article
in *Sports Illustrated* about a pitcher with a 168-mph fastball. It was the talk of
the sports world until someone finally noticed the issue's publication date of
April 1st. I was in high school at the time and our physics teacher spent a whole
class trying to analyze if a human arm could stand the stress of a pitch at that
speed. Enjoy the antics of Sidd and his girlfriend Debbie Sue in this funny and
delightful baseball fairy tale.

Pressfield, Steven
🎬 *The Legend of Bagger Vance: A Novel of Golf and the Game of Life.* 1996
(1995). Avon Books/Spike, ISBN 9780688140489. 272p.

Fictional golfer Rannulph Junah battles his memories of The Great War while trying to rekindle his golf prowess and represent his town in a grand golf match with actual historical champions Bobby Jones and Walter Hagen. Along comes a mysterious stranger who offers to caddy for Junah and straighten out his game and his state of mind. Magical realism at its best, Pressfield deftly intertwines golf, history, and a glorious setting to create a page-turning adventure of self-discovery. He also reinforces the thing that most golfers realize sooner or later: the biggest hurdle to "winning" golf is not the competition, it's you.

Smiley, Jane
Horse Heaven. 2000. Knopf, ISBN 9780375406003. 576p.

Arguably one of the best living American novelists, Smiley provides an entertaining look at the world of championship horse racing, breeding, and the magic of the thoroughbred. Delve inside the minds of horses and humans alike as they strive to reach the pinnacle of their sport. Anything can happen in this ambitious novel that examines all the grand characters of horse racing: trainers, owners, riders, and most importantly the horses themselves. You don't have to be a racing enthusiast to enjoy this finely crafted novel. Find yourself a mint julep and enjoy. ★

Interviews—The Best Questions Asked and Answered

A good interview offers fans deeper insight into the minds and motivations of athletes and coaches. Emphasis on "good" here, because what we read on average in our daily newspapers or websites are mostly boring, monosyllabic interviews. But a good or great interview can enlighten and entertain and be of itself beautifully written. The best interviewers ask thoughtful and informed questions. Sometimes, they just sit back and let their subjects talk. Many former athletes and celebrities like to talk and reminisce. It is time for us to relax and enjoy their recollections.

Holtzman, Jerome
No Cheering in the Press Box. 1995 (1974). Henry Holt & Co., ISBN 978805038231. 363p.

All of the sports writers interviewed in Holtzman's book were writing during what the author calls "the Golden Age of Sports." This was the time between the two World Wars when the likes of Red Smith and Jimmy Cannon were covering the sports beat for their local newspapers. Though all were getting up in age, they had lucid memories of writing about the players, games, and matches that defined their time.

Kilmeade, Brian

The Games Do Count: America's Best and Brightest on the Power of Sports. 2005 (2004). It Books, ISBN 9780060736767. 352p.

The cohost of the popular television morning show *Fox & Friends* interviews 75 business leaders, politicians, celebrities, and athletes and asks them about the influence of sports on their lives. Condoleezza Rice, Jon Stewart, Joan Lunden, and Jon Bon Jovi illustrate the varied backgrounds that Kilmeade include in his book. An interesting peek at how a particular moment or achievement in athletics can affect people throughout their lives. Kilmeade also published another book of interviews in 2007: *It's How You Play the Game: The Powerful Sports Moments That Taught Lasting Values to America's Finest.*

McCullough, Bob

My Greatest Day in Football. 2002 (2001). St Martin's Griffin, ISBN 9780312302962. 288p. [Y][A]

Journalist McCullough has written other books around the same premise including *My Greatest Day in NASCAR* and *My Greatest Day in Golf.* Here he turns his attention to football as he crisscrosses the country in search of legendary football players. The subjects are refreshingly candid and often their memories go beyond a single game or moment to include thoughts on the sport and life itself. Bart Starr, Frank Gifford, and Raymond Berry are only a few of the players interviewed. A feast for football fans.

Ritter, Lawrence

▶ *The Glory of Their Times: The Story of the Early Days of Baseball by the Men Who Played It.* 2010 (1966). Harper Perennial Modern Classics, ISBN 9780061994715. 384p.

One of the seminal books of its kind, this classic collection by author Ritter is a treasure for fans of old-time baseball. What makes the book so unique is that it is told almost entirely by the players as they reminisce about their careers, the players they competed against, and the times themselves. Most of the players featured played in the late 1800s through the early 20th century. Some were quite famous, others not. Their voices come through loud and clear and will leave the reader pining for not only a less complicated age of baseball but also a simpler time for us all.

Trucks, Rob

Cup of Coffee: The Very Short Careers of Eighteen Major League Pitchers. 2002. Smallmouth Press, ISBN 9781588480392, 430p.

Trucks's book is unique because it consists of interviews with baseball pitchers who were only in the big leagues for a very short time, less than 50 innings pitched. What we learn is that their stories are as interesting as some of the superstars of the game. And what a fine line there is between success and failure. And that success and failure can be measured in ways that aren't so obvious. The book looks at the human side of sports and in doing so gives us a new way to appreciate the determination and sacrifice that go into reaching even the periphery of success in the major leagues and surely any sport.

Wilbon, Michael and Charles Barkley
Who's Afraid of a Large Black Man. 2005. Penguin, ISBN 9781615579839. 272p.
  Charles Barkley interviews Barack Obama, Bill Clinton, Morgan Freeman, and other prominent individuals on the topic of race and racism in the United States. Not a sports book at all, but an informative, eye-opening look at the problems and possible solutions to what Barkley calls "the cancer of his lifetime."

Diaries . . . A Day in the Life

There is no writing more personal and intimate than the diary. Day to day, these writers share their deepest emotions, desires, and reservations about the game they love. Some, like Jerry Kramer's *Instant Replay*, harken us back to a simpler day. The stress to succeed is still there, but it is overshadowed by camaraderie and grace. Others tend to be a bit more critical of their fellow players, owners, and the culture of the game, but that desire to be the best is never far from the surface.

Bouton, Jim
Ball Four: My Life and Hard Times Throwing the Knuckleball in the Big Leagues. 1990 (1970). Wiley, ISBN 9780020306658. 456p.
  Today there are very few secrets about professional sports. The Internet, smart phones, and an endless stream of Tweets allow both fans and critics nearly unlimited access to players. Not so in 1970, when Bouton first published his groundbreaking diary about a year in baseball pitching for the Seattle Pilots and Houston Astros. Bouton's remarks about his time with the Yankees, the antics of players, and the state of the game brought him acclaim, but he also was practically blacklisted by the league. A new epilogue is added to this 20th anniversary edition. ★

Hayhurst, Dirk
▶ *The Bullpen Gospels: Major League Dreams of a Minor League Veteran.* 2010. Citadel Press, ISBN 9780806531434. 340p.
  Hayhurst, who only appeared in 25 major league games, has a gift for describing the life of a *not*-top baseball prospect. Self-deprecating, witty, and intelligently written, Hayhurst isn't out to expose anything, rather he writes about his struggles and triumphs in the game he loves. A grand trip through the minor leagues reminiscent of the film *Bull Durham.*

Kramer, Gerald L. and Dick Schaap
Instant Replay: The Green Bay Diary of Jerry Kramer. 2011 (1968). Anchor, ISBN 9780307743381. 320p.
  Kramer takes readers inside the huddle, inside the locker room, and inside the lives of the 1967 Green Bay Packers from the beginning of the season to their Super Bowl victory. Kramer played offensive guard for the Packers, and he writes about his playing style, the finances of the game, and his fellow players and offers particular insight into the coaching style of Vince Lombardi. ★

Lewis, Carl and Jeffrey Marx
  One More Victory Lap. 1996. Aum Publications, ISBN 9780884970057. 225p.

  This book chronicles one year in the life of the great Track and Field champion. Although he won only 1 gold medal in the 1996 Atlanta Olympics (long jump), Lewis won a total of 10 medals in the Olympics alone. Written as a diary, Lewis offers personal insight into his determination to be the best, examines his prospects for the future, and inspires athletes by his actions and reputation. Unfortunately, his later race against Ben Johnson was not so inspirational.

Shirley, Paul
  Can I Keep My Jersey?: 11 Teams, 5 Countries, and 4 Years in My Life as a Basketball Vagabond. 2007. Villard, ISBN 9780345491367. 336p.

  Not all professional athletes live the life of luxury with personal trainers, chefs, accountants, and endorsement deals. Someone must be at the bottom of the ladder of professionals and Shirley is a great standard bearer for professional athletes just trying to stay in the game. Follow Shirley's travels as he writes about life as a journeyman ballplayer. He writes colorfully and candidly about the places he visits and the people he meets. ★

Spadea, Vince and Dan Markowitz
  Break Point! The Secret Diary of a Pro Tennis Player. 2006. Sports Publishing Inc., ISBN 9781596703247. 192p.

  Spadea writes about his 2005 season on the pro tennis tour. Not quite an expose, Spadea does have comments about fellow players and some harsh words regarding Davis Cup coach Patrick McEnroe, but he mainly describes his experience both on and off the court with candor and humor. Groomed to play tennis from age eight, Spadea had a successful tennis career, but as his writing intimates, he may have wanted it to be a little better.

The "A" Team—Anthologies

These collections of sports writing comprise some of the most famous writers of both sports and nonsports. They include fiction and nonfiction and the diversity of sports covered is downright astounding. The titles speak for themselves and we only make one small suggestion about this most impressive list: Enjoy!

Dawidoff, Nicholas
  Baseball: A Literary Anthology. 2002. Library of America, ISBN 9781931082099. 721p.

  This anthology on baseball writing is one of the best and most comprehensive ever compiled. Dawidoff does a fine job mixing poetry, prose, fiction, and sports writing. There are exalted writers from Ring Lardner to Philip Roth to Richard Ford. There are wonderful portraits of Babe Ruth, Satchel Paige, and

Hank Aaron. From *Casey at the Bat* to Giamatti's *Green Fields of the Mind*, this will appeal to any baseball fan and also those who enjoy the fine art of writing. ★

Remnick, David, editor
The Only Game in Town: Sportswriting from the New Yorker. 2010. Random House, ISBN 9781400068029. 512p.

We all know that the *New Yorker* magazine has been home to many fine writers for over 80 years. Their fiction is well known as being top-notch. What is not as well known is the quality of their sports writing. Writers from John Updike to John Cheever have contributed articles on sports and many of them are classics. Add in David Remnick and Roger Angell, who are more known for sports, and you have an exemplary collection that will provide hours of reading pleasure. Also throw in Calvin Trillin on snowmobiling, Henry Louis Gates Jr. on Michael Jordan, and Susan Orlean on dogsledding and put out the "Do Not Disturb" sign. ★

Sandoz, Joli and Joby Winans
Whatever It Takes: Women on Women's Sport. 1999. Farrar, Straus, and Giroux, ISBN 9780374525972. 352p.

What does it mean to be a sportswoman? From the earliest women in professional sports to contemporary athletes in a post–Title IX era, female writers explore the motivations, experiences, and emotions associated with participation in athletics in a society that historically hasn't supported women in sports. Many sports and topics are discussed including cycling, swimming, basketball, and baseball; and the stories passionately show how sport has gained its rightful place in the lives of women and girls in society.

Starr, Jason
Bloodlines: A Horse Racing Anthology. 2006. Vintage, ISBN 978400096954. 372p.

This literary tribute to one of our favorite sports covers everything from jockeys and breeders to bookies and gamblers. The broad range of contributors consists of authors Lee Child, Laura Lippman, Meghan O'Rourke, and many others. The book includes works of fiction and nonfiction and is rich in color and character. We're betting most will love it.

Stevenson, Matthew and Michael Martin
Rules of the Game: The Best Sports Writing from Harper's Magazine. 2010. Franklin Square Press, ISBN 9781879957589. 336p.

Harper's has been writing about the "sporting life" since its inception in 1850 and this compilation of articles represents the best in its distinguished history. We get Mark Twain on "Hunting the Deceitful Turkey," Shirley Jackson on "It's Only a Game," and Wilfred Sheed on "Find Me a Writer." From jogging to our general obsession with sports, there is enough diversity to appeal to any sports or literary fan.

Stout, Glenn and David Halberstam, editors
▶ *The Best American Sportswriting of the Century.* 1999. Mariner Books, ISBN 9780395945148. 816p.

Published since the early 1990s, the editors do a superb job tackling the best of the century. From Grantland Rice to Thomas Wolfe to Hunter S. Thompson, these are major writers authoring some of the greatest sports stories ever written. The diversity of sports covered is astounding and there is something for everyone.

Poetry and Other Shorts

Poetry in motion has been used to describe graceful athletes throughout time. The gracefulness of a well-turned double play or the toughness and speed of a powerful running back are considered poetic by fans and writers. Poems, essays, and ruminations on sport and competition resonate with readers and bring to life the art on the field, court, rink, or pitch. So let's celebrate the poets, comedians, and essayists who immortalize the game with their words.

Abbott, Bud, Lou Costello, and John Martz, illustrator
Who's on First. 2013 (1944). Quirk Books, ISBN 9781594745904. 40p.

A classic comedy sketch that has been performed countless times by baseball fans of all ages is wonderfully illustrated into a colorful children's story. Vivid drawings and clear dialogue bubbles are a delight to read alone or acted out with a partner. This may be a children's book, but give it a try and you will find yourself giggling uncontrollably as you perform a timeless classic.

Davis, Todd
Fast Break to Line Break: Poets on the Art of Basketball. 2012. Michigan State University Press, ISBN 9781611860351. 234p.

Davis wants to challenge the assertion that baseball reigns supreme in writing and poetry. He collects essays from acclaimed present-day poets to discuss the intersection of poetry and basketball. Fluidity, practice, character, and rhythm represent both poets and basketball alike. You may not recognize the names of modern poets, but reading about poets talking about Bird, Johnson, Jordan, and James is mesmerizing.

Dawidoff, Nicholas
▶ *Baseball: A Literary Anthology.* 2002. Library of America, ISBN 9781931082099. 721p.

This title was so good we felt the need to use it twice in this section. Along with classics like *Casey at the Bat*, there are several modern poets and an essay by Robert Frost. A one-stop shop for baseball readers, Dawidoff includes oral histories, interviews from the likes of Ring Lardner, and more modern writers like John Updike. A hefty tome, but worth the effort. ★

Kennedy, Michael P.J.

Going Top Shelf: An Anthology of Canadian Hockey Poetry. 2005. Heritage House Publishing Company Ltd., ISBN 9781894384995. 112p.

Hockey is woven into the culture of Canada like baseball is in America. A professor of literature and writer, Kennedy pulls together poetry and song lyrics that exemplify a nation's love for their game. From the back of the book: ". . . poets are assuming their duty to our great game." It includes a bibliography of hockey literature.

Lincer, Mark Vincent

A Soccer Life in Shorts. 2011. Leftback Publishing LLC, ISBN 9780615466439. 84p. [Y][A]

Lincer entertains readers with this slim volume of vignettes and poems about his life in soccer. From receiving his first yellow card at age eight through his trials and successes on the pitch, Lincer writes with humor and wit about a game that he played for over three decades. With its light tone and short format, this volume has appeal to YA audiences.

Maggs, Randall

Night Work: The Sawchuk Poems. 2008. Brick Books, ISBN 9781894078627. 189p.

For those not familiar with Randall Maggs, he was a goalie for 21 seasons and a benchmark by which other goalies are measured. In this haunting and striking work, Maggs, a poet and literature professor, vividly describes Sawchuk, hockey games, and evokes the feeling and passion of a great goalie and a tortured soul.

Rizzuto, Phil

Oh Holy Cow!: The Selected Verse of Phil Rizzuto. 2008. Ecco, ISBN 9780061567131. 177p.

Hall of Fame shortstop for the New York Yankees, Phil Rizzuto stepped from behind the plate to behind the microphone and enjoyed announcing games for the next 40 years. Called the "Bard of the Booth," Rizzuto was known for his impromptu verse, enthusiastic delivery, and reputation for rooting for the Yankees while broadcasting games. Collected here is the poetry of "The Scooter" with detailed game descriptions. It includes a new poem by the editors and a forward by Bobby Murcer.

Thayer, Ernest and Christopher Bing, illustrator

Casey at the Bat: A Ballad of the Republic Sung in the Year 1888. 2000. Chronicle Books, ISBN 9781929766000. 32p. [Y][A]

There are many versions of this classic baseball poem, but this special edition was selected as a Caldecott Honor book. Lush illustrations create the nostalgic background of an old newspaper and illustrator Bing adds reproductions of baseball cards, ticket stubs, and other memorabilia. Thayer's classic poem comes to life on the page and will be enjoyed by fans no matter the age.

Playwrights Play Right—Broadway and Sports

When we decided to use August Wilson's *Fences* as an example of literary work in the field of sports, we thought we would explore theatrical works to see if there were enough notable titles to make a category. The website Newsday. com "Sports and Broadway" provided a good list of plays and we consulted the Internet Broadway Database (www.ibdb.com) for information on dates and awards. Eric Simonson recently wrote a play called *Magic/Bird (2012)* that is based on the two famed basketball players' relationship. No edition of the play is currently available.

Greenberg, Richard
Take Me Out: A Play. 2002. Faber and Faber, ISBN 9780571211180. 128p.

This original play made its debut on Broadway in 2003 and won the Tony Award for best play of the year. Darren Lemming is a standout ballplayer for a fictional baseball team known as the Empires. The plot revolves around his "coming out" as a gay man and the interactions and opinions of his teammates and others around him.

Maraniss, David
When Pride Still Mattered: A Life of Vince Lombardi. 1999. Simon and Schuster, ISBN 9780684844183. 544p.

In 2010, Maraniss's book was adapted into a Broadway play (*Lombardi*) by Eric Simonson and follows Lombardi through the narration of *Look Magazine* reporter Michael McCormick. The players don't want McCormick around, but through a series of stories and flashbacks, he gets his story and learns his own lessons along the way. ★

Miller, Jason
That Championship Season. 1998 (1974). Dramatists Play Service, ISBN 9780822211266. 72p.

This play won multiple Tony Awards and a Pulitzer prize for drama. Fifteen years after winning the high school basketball championship, five friends visit their coach's house to celebrate the occasion. The players once idolized their coach, but as the liquor flows and the night wears on, the not-so-pleasant realities muddy the delusions of their youth. ★

Odetts, Clifford
Golden Boy: Acting Edition. 1998. Dramatists Play Service, ISBN 9780822204565. 72p.

First performed in 1937, main character Joe Bonaparte must decide whether he wants to become a professional boxer or, of all things, a violinist. Sammy Davis Jr. played Bonaparte in a 1960s musical version of the play, and it played on Broadway in a revival at the Belasco Theatre in late 2012.

Wallop, Douglass

The Year the Yankees Lost the Pennant. 2004 (1954). W.W. Norton and Company, ISBN 9780393326109. 256p.

The Broadway version of this popular novel is better known as *Damn Yankees* and it first played on Broadway in 1955. Joe Boyd makes a deal with the devil in order to help his beloved Washington Senators win the pennant. Joe must succeed before September 21st or his soul will be lost forever. And as we are all aware, the devil is not known to play fair.

Chapter Five

Mood

There is no shortage of emotion in sports. Players, coaches, and fans alike share the elation that follows victory, the sorrow and pain that follows a loss. Many of the titles here are not directly about the games, rather the authors examine larger issues that surround us all: friendships, success in life, remembrance, sacrifice, and faith. While we avoid regional titles throughout this book, we took a little license and offer a prime list relating to the futility of being a Cleveland Browns' fan—that's us.

Before the Fall . . .

Great athletes, impeccable personalities, loved by all, and without fault, these folks took a turn for the worse with regard to public opinion. Annotations here follow the plot and themes of beloved players and coaches. Keep in mind that the companion category that follows does not look kindly on said players and coaches. Reading the corresponding titles back to back may cause dizziness, depression, and incredulousness. We had originally placed Jim Tressel here, but there are no books speaking out against his NCAA violations. Compared to others in the category, his missteps seem almost trivial.

Armstrong, Lance
▶ *It's Not About the Bike: My Journey Back to Life.* 2001. Berkley Trades, ISBN 9780425179611. 304p.
   This book attracted a huge readership due to the inspirational message of determination and triumph as Armstrong fought through testicular cancer to

become one of the greatest cyclists in history. Written the year he won his third Tours de France (seven total), Armstrong reflects on cycling, friends and family, and a journey that a few years later spawned a rash of yellow bracelets on wrists throughout the world.

Fitzpatrick, Frank

Pride of the Lions: The Biography of Joe Paterno. 2011. Triumph Books, ISBN 9781600786150. 256p.

With a total of 62 years as a Penn State coach including 44 years as head coach, Paterno has the longest tenure of any coach at the Division I level. Published only months before the scandal that rocked Happy Valley, this book presents the best of "JoePa" from his Brooklyn roots to his legendary coaching career.

Fox, Larry

The O.J. Simpson Story: Born to Run. 1974. Dodd, Mead, ISBN 9780396070092. 173p. Y A

Ok, this one is a stretch. Poor Orenthal James Simpson played before the proliferation of memoirs and biographies previous to old age. WorldCat shows this YA title in over 250 libraries, so it's the winner. This title chronicles the life of a young man born to poverty who went on to fame at USC and later the Buffalo Bills. In 1973, he became the first NFL player to surpass 2,000 yards rushing in a season.

Heller, Peter

Bad Intentions: The Mike Tyson Story. 1995 (1989). Da Capo Press, ISBN 9780306806698. 476p.

It's hard to believe from the title that this is the "before" title we found for Iron Mike Tyson. Part biography and part boxing history, Heller adds a postscript in the 1995 edition. The first edition of this title was published before Tyson went to prison; the latest edition was released in 1995 and so was Mike. Unfortunately, his imprisonment wasn't "the fall."

Kearns, Brian

How Tiger Does It. 2008. McGraw Hill, ISBN 9780071545648. 208p.

While at the top of his game, Tiger could do no wrong. Kearns reveals how Tiger's mastery at golf can transfer to success in life. Focus, work-play ethic, and a balanced approach are the philosophies of his success. Ironically, Kearns also wrote a book titled *How Lance Does It*. Oh Brother! See also *Follow the Roar: Tailing Tiger for All 604 Holes of His Most Spectacular Season* (2008) by Bob Smiley.

Posnanski, Joe

The Machine: A Hot Team, a Legendary Season, and a Heart Stopping World Series: The Story of the 1975 Cincinnati Reds. 2010 (2009). Harper Paperbacks, ISBN 9780061582554. 302p.

Pete Rose played an essential role in the Reds championship season. This book may be only partly about him, but it shows Rose in his glory with fellow teammates and offers readers a glimpse of an amazing player at the top of his game. In 1975, *Sports Illustrated* named Rose their "Sportsman of the Year."

Rapoport, Ron
See How She Runs: Marion Jones and the Making of a Champion. 2000. Algonquin Books, ISBN 9781565122673. 224p. Y A

She won four gold medals at the 1999 World Track and Field Championships and was on her way to multiple gold medals at the Sydney Olympics. Billed as the next great track superstar, Jones offers complete access to Rapoport, providing an intimate look at the struggles, triumphs, and adversity as this talented multisport athlete focuses on track and field. Well, there may have been a secret.

. . . After the Fall

Great athletes, flawed personalities, but still they go on.

Bugliosi, Vincent
Outrage: The Five Reasons Why O.J. Simpson Got Away with Murder. 1996. W. W. Norton and Company, ISBN 9780393040500. 368p.

Bugliosi prosecuted Charles Manson, so he has some experience in high-profile cases. Here he breaks down the prosecutorial missteps and offers his opinions on the trial of a beloved football hero fallen from grace. Bugliosi has publicly stated that there is no doubt Simpson was guilty and here he explains the why and how. It includes the complete LAPD interrogation of O.J. and other indices.

Hamilton, Tyler et. al 🏆
The Secret Race: Inside the Hidden World of the Tour de France: Doping, Cover-ups, and Winning at All Costs. 2012. Bantam Books, ISBN 9780593071748. 304p.

Hamilton rode with Lance Armstrong and was one of his most trusted lieutenants, helping him win his first three Tour de France titles. He passionately writes about the pressures of tour racing and the need to change the culture of professional cycling. Hamilton takes Armstrong and others to task about doping, and he also implicates himself in the whole mess. A sad statement on the affairs of cycling.

Jones, Marion
On the Right Track: From Olympic Downfall to Finding Forgiveness and the Strength to Overcome and Succeed. 2010. Howard Books, ISBN 9781451626308. 240p.

The one time "fastest woman on the planet" took a meteoric fall in 2007 when she had to return her Olympic medals after admitting taking performance-enhancing drugs. The downward spiral continued as she was sentenced to a short prison term for check fraud. However, Jones has rebounded from her troubles and offers a cautionary message about the pressures to succeed and an inspirational message of finding the right path for life.

Lusetich, Robert
Unplayable: An Inside Account of Tiger's Most Tumultuous Season. 2010. Atria Books, ISBN 9781439160954. 269p.

Lusetich follows Tiger through every agonizing hole of 2009. Fresh from rehab on his repaired knee, Tiger could not return immediately to his old form and struggles mightily throughout the season, and his problems are multiplied when his transgressions off the course cause greater problems than a bum knee. We don't have a "During the Fall" category, but this title would fit well there. Today, Tiger has regained his number one status in golf, but his reputation is still on the rebound.

O'Connor, Daniel, editor.
Iron Mike: A Tyson Reader. 2002. Da Capo Press, ISBN 9781560253563. 336p.

Famed sports writer George Plimpton forwards this collection of articles and essays documenting the rise, fall, rise, and fall again of once heavyweight champion Mike Tyson. Joyce Carol Oates leads off the book with a 1987 piece about Mike's tumultuous upbringing and rise to the title. The last article is from 2002 and Tyson's roller-coaster life is still on the rails. In November 2013, Tyson is due to publish his autobiography *Undisputed Truth*.

Posnanski, Joe
▶ *Paterno.* 2012. Simon and Schuster, ISBN 9781451657494. 416p.

The definitive biography on Joe Paterno, this book chronicles the life of coach from his early days in Brooklyn through the scandal that will forever change his legacy. Posnanski had access to Paterno's private papers and includes a useful bibliography containing a host of titles published throughout Paterno's life. A three-dimensional portrait of a life of a great coach, mentor, and fallible human being.

Rose, Pete and Rick Hill
My Prison without Bars. 2004. Rodale Books, ISBN 9781579549275. 336p.

Three World Series wins, 17 MVP awards, voted one of the top 100 baseball players of the century. Gambling problems, perhaps a mental disorder, jail time. The two sides of Pete Rose are polar opposites and fans will argue the merits of his being reinstated to baseball for a long time to come. Here he talks about his early life, discusses his troubles, and finally admits to gambling on the Reds—to win, never to lose. A fascinating first-person account of a defiant and unapologetic man.

Good Advice, Great Coaches

Championship coaches sometimes transcend their fields. John Wooden's Pyramid of Success (http://www.coachwooden.com/pyramidpdf.pdf) was a revolutionary model that crossed over from sports, business, and life. Below are some other men and women whose coaching philosophies have moved beyond the field of athletics and they provide valuable advice and guidance no matter the endeavor. Professional football and college basketball coaches are prolific writers of leadership books, while hockey and baseball coaches not so much.

Dungy, Tony
Quiet Strength: The Principles, Practices, and Priorities of a Winning Life. 2008 (2007). Tyndale Momentum, ISBN 9781414318028. 352p.

Dungy doesn't go for yelling and berating his players. He believes in respect, hard work, family, and a strong belief in God. Follow his story as this Super Bowl winning coach explains his faith, his coaching philosophy, and his view that a coach should be a teacher, not a bully. A devout man, Dungy's faith plays a prominent role throughout.

Harrity, Mike
▶ *Coaching Wisdom: Champion Coaches and Their Players Share Successful Leadership Principles: How Tony Dungy, Lou Holtz, Andrea Hudy, Don Shula, John Wooden, and Other Top Coaches Inspired Their Teams to Greatness.* 2012. Sellers, ISBN 978141620655. 192p.

Great coaches inspire their players to greatness. Harrity profiles coaches and their leadership styles, focusing on attributes that can transfer to everyday life. Former players support the stories and the author adds his own insight to create a quality title that is valuable to coaches, players, and nonathletes alike.

Jackson, Phil
Sacred Hoops: Spiritual Lessons of a Hardwood Warrior. 2006 (1995). Hyperion, ISBN 9781401308810. 240p.

Jackson originally wrote this book when he only had three NBA titles under his belt. He offers his insights for success and leadership using a unique combination of Eastern philosophy and Native American spiritual practice. Part memoir, part inspirational, and part educational, Jackson's beliefs can help foster success on and off the court. For an updated look at his life in basketball, check out his new book *Eleven Rings: The Soul of Success* (2013).

Knight, Bobby and Bob Hammel
The Power of Negative Thinking. 2013. New Harvest, ISBN 9780544027718. 240p.

The second winningest coach in NCAA basketball, Knight certainly doesn't follow the philosophy of Tony Dungy! Minimizing vulnerabilities, practicing for every conceivable failure, and not dwelling on success are just some of the pragmatic lessons offered by this one-of-a-kind coach.

Russell, Bill
Russell Rules: 11 Lessons on Leadership from the Twentieth Century's Greatest Winner. 2002 (2001). New American Library, ISBN 9780451203885. 244p.

Eleven NBA titles in 13 seasons: he must have been doing something right. Russell lays out his rules for success in business, life, and, to a lesser extent, sports. Curiosity, commitment, and craftsmanship are a few of traits that he attributes to success. Each rule has a set of subrules, so there is lots of advice packed in this timeless volume.

Sullivan, Steve
▄ *Remember This Titan: The Bill Yoast Story: Lessons Learned from a Celebrated Coach's Journey as Told to Steve Sullivan.* 2007 (2005). Taylor Trade Publishing, ISBN 9781589793361. 153p.

Bill Yoast was the head football coach of T. C. Williams High School in Virginia until the team was integrated in 1972. Yoast became an assistant coach to his replacement, Herman Boone, and together they led the team to a state championship. Yoast offers coaching philosophy and life philosophy as he takes most pride in the accomplishments of his players after they left high school.

Summit, Pat
Reach for the Summit. 1998. Three Rivers Press, ISBN 9780767902298. 288p.

The winningest coach in NCAA basketball history only had five championships at the time of publication. Here she explains her "Definite Dozen" principles for success. Every successful group needs people, system, communication, work ethic, and discipline, and Pat adds humor and conviction to the stories that detail her philosophy.

Walsh, Bill, Steve Jamison, and Craig Walsh
The Score Takes Care of Itself: My Philosophy on Leadership. 2009. Portfolio Hardcover, ISBN 9781591842668. 288p.

Winner of three Super Bowls in the 1980s, Walsh core leadership principles focused on ethics, teaching, and performance. Published after his death, his son Craig and coauthor Jamison use Bill's notes and interviews with players to compile a noteworthy account that will benefit leaders in all fields. ★

Nostalgia—The Good Old Days

Many pro athletes often refer with respect to "Old School" athletes, and commentators and fans love to revel in "the good old days." Before free agency and multimillion dollar contracts, before dream teams and chosen ones, before endorsements and pay-per-view, there were just the games. Rebellious, quaint, and sometimes reckless, this is the way it was done in the past.

Araton, Harvey

When the Garden Was Eden: Clyde, the Captain, Dollar Bill, and the Glory Days of the New York Knicks. 2011. Harper, ISBN 9780061956232. 351p.

In the late 1960s and early 1970s, the New York Knicks reigned supreme. Walt "Clyde" Frazier, Willis Reed, and Bill Bradley brought their magnificent games to Madison Square Garden every night and the city of New York was enthralled. The ongoing Vietnam War and general social unrest of the time serve as a backdrop to Araton's book and he expertly takes us back to that time to that city where a true "team" competed and played the game the way it should be played.

Corcoran, Dennis

Induction Day at Cooperstown: A History of the Baseball Hall of Fame Ceremony. 2010. McFarland, ISBN 9780786444168. 282p.

To a baseball fan, all you have to do is say "Cooperstown" and they'll know what you mean. Each year all eyes focus on this small town to see who is inducted into the Baseball Hall of Fame. Why Cooperstown? Who's in and why? This concise volume includes biographies of past recipients, quotes from speeches, and fascinating facts about the greats of the game all relating to their entrance into the Hall of Fame.

Leershen, Charles

Blood and Smoke: A True Tale of Mystery, Mayhem and the Birth of the Indy 500. 2011. Simon and Schuster, ISBN 9781439149041. 288p.

Leershen gives readers a front row seat to the running of the first Indianapolis 500 automobile race in 1911. At the time, some viewed racing as too violent and that its appeal was in the ultimate destruction of cars and drivers. Political intrigue, power struggles, and larger-than-life characters populate this historical romp through the beginnings of one of today's most notable and prestigious race venues in the world. ★

McKinley, Michael

Hockey: A People's History. 2009 (2006). McClelland and Stewart, ISBN 9780771057717. 384p.

A companion book to a popular Canadian Broadcasting Company miniseries, this wonderfully illustrated volume guides readers from the conception of hockey in 1875 through to today's modern game. The fun is in the history, as McKinley writes of topics such as the early leagues, the dilemma of women's hockey, the evolution of a sport, and the men and women that makes it so popular today. ★

Murphy, Cait

Crazy '08: How a Cast of Cranks, Rogues, Boneheads, and Magnates Created the Greatest Year in Baseball History. 2007. Smithsonian, ISBN 9780060889371. 384p.

Murphy brings to life the memorable and outrageous events of the 1908 pennant race between the Tigers, Cubs, and New York (baseball) Giants. Immortal characters like Ty Cobb and Honus Wagner, historical ball fields such as The Polo Grounds, and the drama and frenzy of a public consumed by baseball are vividly drawn and well researched in this highly readable work. ★

Nicholson, James

▶ *The Kentucky Derby: How the Run for the Roses Became America's Premier Sporting Event.* 2012. The University Press of Kentucky, ISBN 9780813135762. 296p.

All eyes turn to Kentucky the first Saturday in May to witness a few minutes of awe-inspiring horse racing. There are few settings as iconic as Churchill Downs. The history and pageantry are all here, as well as the cultural and political perspective. As the author notes, a "Derby" is the term used for a race of three-year-old thoroughbreds; and Kentucky, with its rich history and pageantry, is what makes this race special.

Thompson, Neal

Driving with the Devil: Southern Moonshine, Detroit Wheels, and the Birth of NASCAR. 2007 (2006). Broadway Books, ISBN 9781400082261. 432p.

One of the most popular sports in America today, NASCAR's origins in the 1930s and 1940s have roots in bootleggers trying to design cars to outmaneuver law enforcement. Learn about racing pioneer Raymond Parks and a colorful cast of whiskey runners, and how Bill France wrested control and changed the sport to its current form. Thompson got a firsthand account from Parks, who at 91 years old is one of the last living bootleg racers. Plus, how could a story with such colorful characters as Pee Wee, Jocco, Hooker, Pig Iron, or Blackie not be entertaining.

Fans or Fanatics?

We salute those of you who paint your homes the color of your favorite team (except pinstripes). We salute those of you who plan your schedules around your favorite sports teams. There is no room for fair-weather fans here. This section is for true fans that live and die with their teams. As two Cleveland sports fans, we understand your pain, but we don't get the elation part so much. Much to our dismay, we also felt compelled to add another Boston book in our lists even though we did not want to. *Fever Pitch* by Nick Hornby is a delightful book and 1997 film about the obsession of a soccer fan, but the 2005 movie featured the Boston Red Sox . . . ugh.

Costas, Bob

Fair Ball: A Fan's Case for Baseball. 2001 (2000). Broadway Books, ISBN 9780767904667. 197p.

Well known for his compelling interview style and competent reporting, Costas makes his case for changes to baseball for the betterment of the game.

Since its publication in 2000, there have been many changes and issues in baseball that he approached in his book. What makes this book most interesting is
comparing what Costas wrote then to the state of the game today.

Hornby, Nick
▶ 🎬 *Fever Pitch*. 2010 (1992). Riverhead Books, ISBN 9781573226882. 239p.
   Hornby's life through the lens of soccer and his favorite team the Arsenal
Gunners is both funny and at times disturbing. The book tracks his lifelong
obsession with soccer, and it was made into a popular American film starring
Drew Barrymore and Jimmy Fallon using the Boston Red Sox as the "favorite"
team. There is also a 1997 film starring Colin Firth. ★

Milano, Alyssa
Safe at Home: Confessions of a Baseball Fanatic. 2010 (2009). It Books, ISBN
   9780061625114. 241p.
   Popular television and film star Milano sets her sites on baseball in this
insightful look on her life as a Dodgers fan first and a baseball fan most of all.
She offers tips to help novices understand the game, opinions on the state of
baseball, and intimate stories of growing up watching baseball with her dad.
Her candid and conversational style is entertaining and easy to read.

Queenan, Joe
True Believers: The Tragic Inner Life of Sports Fans. 2004 (2003). Picador,
   ISBN 9780312423216. 256p.
   Queenan believes that his 18-year "foul mood" is brought on by the fact
that the sports teams he roots for have not won a championship in that time.
He takes a look at why fan's root tirelessly for their teams, some of who have
never won a championship—ever. As Cleveland fans ourselves, we don't have
to read this book because we understand Queenan's premise quite well. ★

Robinson Peete, Holly and Daniel Paisner
*Get Your Own Damn Beer, I'm Watching the Game!: A Woman's Guide to
   Loving Pro Football.* 2005. Rodale Books, ISBN 9781594861635. 228p.
   Television actress Robinson Peete (*Hangin' with Mr. Cooper*, *21 Jump
Street*, etc.) also happens to be married to former NFL quarterback Rodney
Peete. Here she offers an assist to women who want to understand this bizarre
game with its x's and o's and strange lingo. Supplemented with historical facts
of the game and stories of her growing up an Eagles fan, she provides insight
into the game that would be of use to any fan.

Seely, Hart
*The Juju Rules: Or, How to Win Ballgames from Your Coach: A Memoir of
   a Fan Obsessed.* 2013 (2012). Mariner Books, ISBN 9780544002203. 288p.
   Hart Seely is a Yankees fan, much to the chagrin of his father who always rooted for APY (Anyone Playing the Yankees). In this very funny memoir,

Seely traces the evolution of his fanaticism through stories about baseball and family. And don't forget the Juju: it's not the players or coaches that win games, it's the collective power of thousands of fans focusing on the game.

Simmons, Bill
Now I Can Die in Peace: How the Sports Guy Found Salvation Thanks to the World Champion (Twice!) Red Sox. 2009. Ballantine Books, ISBN 9781933060729. 464p.

> *ESPN The Magazine* columnist and die-hard Boston fan, Simmons compiles 10 years' worth of Red Sox columns in this updated version of the title by the same name. Follow the incredible ups and downs of man obsessed with every move of his beloved team. The book is laced with his trademark humor, pop culture sidebars, and historical tidbits. Read Queenan then Simmons followed by Seely and you get a pretty good chronology of several types of fans. ★

Winner, David
Brilliant Orange: The Neurotic Genius of Dutch Soccer. 2008 (2002). Overlook TP, ISBN 9781590200551. 288p.

> Anyone who watched the Olympics, summer or winter, has seen the growing enthusiasm for Dutch teams by the fields of orange in the stands. In a new preface by Franklin Foer, he states that many Americans root for Dutch soccer because they like the Netherlands and its liberal and intellectual ideals. Winner attempts to explain the link between Dutch society, culture, and soccer; and how the style of the Dutch game is unique because of this relationship. ★

Fathers and Sons (and Daughters Too)

"Hey Dad . . . You wanna have a catch?" A great line from the movie *Field of Dreams* is the impetus for this category. In today's world, fathers don't have a monopoly on teaching, coaching, and watching sports with their kids, but most of the books we found are about dads and their children. Whether it is watching their children play from the stands, enjoying a game with dad, or fondly remembering the days being taken to the ballpark, these fathers, sons, and daughters remind us of those happy times.

Atkinson, Jay
▶ *Ice Time: A Tale of Fathers, Sons, and Hometown Heroes.* 2002 (2001). Broadway, ISBN 9780609809945. 321p.

> Atkinson shines a light on his hometown and its ties to hockey as he returns home to be assistant coach of the Methuen Mass. Rangers varsity hockey team. While his hopes for the future of his five-year-old son is touching, his vivid descriptions of small-town hockey offer a heartwarming view of sport at its best.

Axelrod, Jim
In the Long Run: A Father, a Son, and Unintentional Lessons in Happiness.
2011. Farrar, Straus and Giroux, ISBN 9780374192112. 304p.

A successful CBS correspondent, Axelrod has traveled the world covering stories from the war in Iraq to presidential politics. This revealing memoir finds Jim at a crossroads as he works too much, drinks too much, and neglects his family for career. He discovers his father's old New York marathon times and decides to not only run the marathon, but also best his father's efforts. Told with graceful style and passionate prose, Axelrod mingles family history with his determination to come to terms with his life and find happiness.

Brennan, Christine
Best Seat in the House: A Father, a Daughter, a Journey through Sports. 2006. Scribner, ISBN 9780743254366. 283p.

Encouraged by her father to play, love, and write about sports, Brennan was the first female sports journalist to join the *Miami Herald* in 1981. She has covered the Olympics and is a respected reporter both in print and on television. Here she describes her childhood in Toledo, Ohio, her early love of sports, and her father who stood by her side the entire time. A loving tribute to Jim Brennan, who passed away in 2003.

Gullo, Jim
Trading Manny: How a Father and Son Learned to Love Baseball Again. 2012. Da Capo Press, ISBN 9780306820175. 255p.

A father and a son recapture their love of baseball in an era of disillusionment due to steroids. Gullo's seven-year-old son asks questions about baseball players and steroids that he cannot answer. So they travel across the country asking questions of players and managers to find the truth. Together, they remove the cards from their collection of known users and come to the difficult understanding that sometimes our heroes are quite flawed human beings.

Kilpatrick, Bill
Brassies, Mashies, and Bootleg Scotch: Growing Up on America's First Heroic Golf Course. 2011. University of Nebraska Press, ISBN 9780803236424. 176p.

An endearing account of growing up as the son of a "greenkeeper" at The National Golf Links of America, written with fondness and affection. His father was born in Scotland and played St. Andrews as a child, but came here to work at America's fledgling golf courses. Kirkpatrick's stories are brimming with interesting characters, nostalgia, and a respect for his demanding but loving father.

Kinsella, W. P.
Shoeless Joe. 1999 (1982). Mariner Books, ISBN 9780395957738. 272p.

While the movie *Field of Dreams* was based on this novel, Kinsella's original story emanates with deeper themes than the film. Ray Kinsella hears a voice that tells him to build a baseball field in the middle of his cornfield, confounding neighbors and the bankers who hold his mortgage. Emotionally vibrant and written with a conversational style, Kinsella explores relationships, trust, family, and redemption in this striking and magical story. ★

Leitch, Will
Are We Winning? Fathers and Sons in the New Golden Age of Baseball. 2010. Hyperion, ISBN 9781401323707. 304p.

    Fathers and sons, beer and baseball, Cubs versus Cardinals; this has the makings of a good day. Leitch tells more than the story of a baseball game as he and his father travel to Wrigley field to watch their Cardinals play. Not concerned with steroid use or the state of baseball today, Leitch reminisces with his father, tells stories of growing up, and has some fun with Dad.

Strauss, Robert
Daddy's Little Goalie: A Father, His Daughters, and Sports. 2011. Andrews McMeel, ISBN 9781449402341. 160p.

    In 1971, at the time of the implementation of Title IX, there were 294,000 girls playing high school sports. In 2011, the number was over 3 million. The explosion in participation has created a whole generation of father's supporting, nurturing, and training their daughters for athletic success. Strauss writes about the sporting life with his daughters Ella and Sylvia through a collection of anecdotes, some funny, some sad, but all emotionally charged by the love of a father.

Remembrance—Lives Cut Short

    Lou Gehrig remarking that he was the luckiest man on earth (see Jonathan Eig's *Luckiest Man: The Life and Death of Lou Gehrig*) or the millions of people who sport Dale Earnhardt's number "3" on the back of their windshields is a testament to how the lives of sports heroes affects us. Unfortunately, these great athletes are only human and can succumb to the same ailments as us mortals. Follow the lives of athletes who left us much too young and witness their extraordinary achievements, their battles, and the heartfelt stories of those who loved them.

Appel, Marty
Munson: The Life and Death of a Yankee Captain. 2009. Doubleday, ISBN 9780385522311. 384p.

    Celebrated Yankee's captain and catcher Thurman Munson died in a plane crash in 1979 while flying home after a game. Appel, a former public relations director for the Yankees, was the ghostwriter for Thurman's autobiography published 30 years ago. In this book, he presents an in-depth and honest look into Munson's early life in Canton, Ohio, and his popularity and success with the 1970s Yankees. ★

Dent, Jim

Courage beyond the Game: The Freddie Steinmark Story. 2011. Thomas Dunne Books, ISBN 9780312652852. 304p.

Dent, who wrote the *Junction Boys* and other great Texas football stories, reveals the life of an exceptional young man who died of bone cancer during the prime of his college football career. Dent chronicles Steinmark's life growing up in Colorado, his popularity and athletic prowess in high school, and his success as a defensive back at the University of Texas. Six days after Texas's historic win over Arkansas in one of the greatest games in college history, Steinmark was diagnosed with cancer. He died at the age of 21. ★

Gallagher, Robert C.

The Express: The Ernie Davis Story. 2008 (1983). Ballantine Books, ISBN 9780345510860. 208p.

He never played a down for the Cleveland Browns, but they retired his jersey (#45) after he ran onto the field one time in 1962. A powerful running back for Syracuse and the first African American to win the Heisman, Davis was slated to share the backfield with Jim Brown until leukemia ended his football career. An authentic hero whose potential can only be imagined, Davis died in 1963 at the age of 24.

Kerig, William

The Edge of Never: A Skier's Story of Life, Death, and Dreams in the World's Most Dangerous Mountains. 2008. Stone Creek Publications, ISBN 9780965633840. 320p.

At age 34, Trevor Peterson, an acclaimed ski mountaineer, died in an avalanche at Chamonix in the French Alps. This story, part memoir and part coming-of-age tale, follows Trevor's son Kyle at just 15 years old, as he re-traces his father's steps and ski's the mountain that took his father's life. Adventure, remembrance, and triumph create a winning combination and insightful read.

Maraniss, David

Clemente: The Passion and Grace of Baseball's Last Hero. 2007 (2006). Simon and Schuster, ISBN 9780743299992. 416p.

Eighteen season with the same team is an astonishing feat when compared to today's players. Roberto Clemente's excellence in baseball pales in comparison to his humanitarian work; he died in a plane crash in 1972 while delivering humanitarian aid to earthquake victims in Nicaragua. Maraniss traces Clemente's story from a poor upbringing in Puerto Rico to his legacy as one of the greats of the game. ★

Pearlman, Jeff

Sweetness: The Enigmatic Life of Walter Payton. 2011. Gotham, ISBN 9781592406531. 479p.

I remember watching Payton's memorial service on television as thousands of fans streamed into Soldier Field to pay homage to a great athlete, devoted father, and generous philanthropist who succumbed to liver cancer in 1999. Beginning with Payton's growing up in the segregated South and ending with a poignant accounting of his legacy, Pearlman's exhaustive research and candid writing is no homage to a superstar, but an honest and thorough accounting of Payton's life.

Reng, Ronald 🏆
▶ *A Life Too Short: The Tragedy of Robert Enke.* 2011. Random House UK, ISBN 9780224091657. 400p.

A deeply tragic story of a world-class German goalkeeper, this book chronicles the life of a man who took his own life after a long battle with depression. Reng was a friend of Enke's and his writing is sensitive and moving as he describes Enke's seemingly successful life, his ultimate demise, and the family, friends, and fans that mourned his loss.

Waltrip, Michael and Ellis Henican
In the Blink of an Eye: Dale, Daytona, and the Day That Changed Everything. 2011. Hyperion, ISBN 9781401324315. 204p.

Waltrip's greatest day turned into his worst day in 2001 when he won the Daytona 500 and Dale Earnhardt Sr., his boss and friend, died in a crash on the final lap of the race. This candid memoir takes readers back to Waltrip's growing up in Kentucky and his nearly 30-year career in NASCAR. Emotional, confessional, and sometimes humorous, Waltrip retells the fateful day at Daytona and explores his own life along the way.

Sports Photography—A Picture Is Worth . . .

Sports photographers capture the gamut of emotions as they freeze a moment in time. From studio shoots to live action shots to behind the scenes images, the selections below offer some of the most spectacular and vivid photographs in a variety of sports. One notable photographer is absent from this list; Walter Iooss Jr. has graced the pages of some 300 *Sports Illustrated* covers, but he has not had a book of note published lately. However, he is worth looking up as he is one of the most iconic American photographers in recent history.

Cameron, Steve, editor and Matthew Manor, photographer
Hockey Hall of Fame Treasures. 2011. Firefly Books, ISBN 9781554078875. 224p.

A highly artistic arrangement of hockey history is gathered in this beautifully designed volume. Over 500 photographs grace the pages telling the story of hockey through the places, players, and even the equipment used throughout the years. Extended captions describe the dazzling photography. If you can't make it to the Hall of Fame, this is the next best thing.

Corporan, Alex, Andre Razo, and Ivory Serra, editors
Full Bleed: New York City Skateboard Photography. 2010. Power House Books, ISBN 9781576875391. 304p.

The editors present a selection of fantastic skateboarding shots taken amid the stunning backdrop of New York City. A cacophony of visual magic bursts from the page as skateboarders weave through traffic, do tricks in parks, and make one giant skate park out of the endless possibilities of the city. All eras of skating are represented in this gritty and beautiful book.

Gottesman, Jane
Game Face: What Does a Female Athlete Look Like. 2003 (2001). Random House Trade Paperbacks, ISBN 9780812968682. 224p. [Y][A]

Penny Marshall writes the introduction and says to girls and women everywhere: "Don't be ashamed of your talent." Gottesman laments the view that women's sports are second rate and provides evidence to the contrary. A wonderful look at female athletes past and present, amateur and professional, she highlights some of the greatest events in female sports and she incorporates black and white photographs from famous photographers who have captured the "game face" of women in sports.

Hewitt, Ian and Bob Martin, editors
Wimbledon: Visions of the Championships. 2011. Visions Sports Publishing, ISBN 9781907637124. 256p.

Witness the oldest tennis tournament in the world from start to finish in this breathtaking collection of photographs from the 2009 tournament. Behind the scenes, outside the stadium, panoramic shots from above, and of course the players are shown in vibrant color. Photographer Bob Martin and writer Ian Hewitt capture the pure Englishness that is Wimbledon and the transformation of the All England Lawn Tennis Club in glorious detail.

Jenkins, Tom
In the Moment: The Sports Photography of Tom Jenkins. 2012. Guardian Books, ISBN 9780852652855. 188p.

England's premier sports photographer selects his finest photographs taken over his 20-year career. Rugby, soccer, fencing, and the Olympics are some of the subjects he brought to life in *The Guardian* and *The Observer*. Vibrant, emotional, and evocative, Jenkins captures the drama of athletics beautifully. While the photographs are the stars here, the captions and an introductory essay offer insight into the making of the shots.

Murray, Arnold, Gabriel Schecter, and Neil Leifer, photographer
Guts and Glory: The Golden Age of American Football. 2011. Taschen, ISBN 9783836527866. 296p.

For over 50 years, Neil Leifer has been capturing moments in sports history. Leifer culls the best of his football photographs taken from 1958 through 1978, from Vince Lombardi and the Packers to Minnesota's Purple People Eaters, and the book contains color and B&W photographs of championships, cheerleaders, and all facets of the game. It seems that football was muddier in the days before artificial turf. Commentary by Jim Murray, Pulitzer prize–winning columnist adds historical context to this pictorial journey.

O'Mahony, Mike
▶ *Olympic Visions: Images of the Games through History.* 2012. Reaktion Books, ISBN 9781861899101. 175p.

British art historian O'Mahoney traces the history of the Olympic Games through every artistic medium. From sculpture and paintings to film and mixed media, the Olympics have been a part of politics, culture, and athletics from the very beginning. O'Mahony's thorough academic research and engaging commentary provides a unique view of the evolution and intertwining of sport and culture.

Schatz, Howard
At the Fights: Inside the World of Professional Boxing. 2012. Sports Illustrated, ISBN 9781618930057. 240p.

Odds are, if you have opened a magazine in the past 20 years or so, you have seen the work of Howard Schatz. Ophthalmologist turned photographer, Schatz spent six years putting together this compendium on the boxing world. Promoters, trainers, announcers, and boxers are portrayed in live action and studio shots. Captions are provided by a host of writers in the boxing world rounding out this intimate and human look at boxing.

At What Cost—The Price of Excellence

Todd Marinovich could be the poster child for what not to do as an elite athlete. His father, Marv, trained him to be a quarterback practically from birth, and he controlled everything about young Todd's diet, social life, and exercise. Unfortunately, the young quarterback didn't fulfill expectations and spiraled into epic failure (*ESPN Films: The Marinovich Project*, 2012). For some, becoming the best requires a true deal with the devil. These unfortunate souls lost more than they gained by striving to be the best and others found success to cost too high a price.

Beard, Amanda and Rebecca Paley
In the Water They Can't See You Cry. 2012. Touchstone, ISBN 9781451644371. 256p.

On the surface, Amanda had a perfect life: Olympic medals, a successful modeling career, and worldwide appeal. However, she also struggled with bulimia, depression, and drug use. She bears all in this thoughtful memoir and describes her recovery through faith and family.

Cleave, Chris
Gold: A Novel. 2012. Simon and Schuster, ISBN 9781451672725. 336p.

Kate and Zoe have been competing against one another for years as track cyclists. Now in their 30s, they are vying for a position on the 2012 Olympic team, but their intense struggles in the velodrome are complicated by life and family. Kate's daughter has leukemia, and the stress of competition might be too much when coupled with caring for her daughter. Zoe is also torn by her need to win and her self-perceived unfair advantage over her rival and friend. ★

Friedman, Steve
▶ *The Agony of Victory: When Winning Isn't Enough.* 2007. Arcade Publishing, ISBN 9781559708517. 288p.

Compiled from articles Friedman wrote over the years, this anthology brings together the "best" of the tortured souls of sports. Physically, they perform at the upper levels of their sport; mentally, they could use an assist. Elite athletes with a singular focus pour over into obsession. Friedman's stories examine what happens when life balance loses out to the need for perfection.

Kriegel, Mark
Pistol: The Life of Peter Maravich. 2008 (2007). Free Press, ISBN 9780743284981. 393p.

Kriegel has an eye for sports stories that capture the demons that invade sports stars. (He wrote a book about Joe Namath too.) Much like Todd Marinovich, Pete's father trained his son for basketball greatness. A player like no other, he had amazing ball skills and scoring ability. Fighting injuries, alcoholism, and depression, Pete's story is a cautionary tale of the drive to be the best. ★

Kriegel, Mark
The Good Son: The Life of Ray "Boom Boom" Mancini. 2012. Free Press, ISBN 9780743286350. 336p.

Inspired by his father to become a boxer, Mancini was born in the shadow of Youngstown Ohio steel mills. A fabulous and positive individual, he rose to WBA lightweight champion in 1981. In a match that would change his life forever, Mancini knocked out Duk Koo Kim; tragically, Kim later died from his injuries. Kriegel writes vividly of Mancini, his upbringing, the "fight," and Boom Boom's life after boxing. ★

Moceanu, Dominique
Off Balance: A Memoir. 2012. Touchstone, ISBN 9781451608656. 256p.

Now 30 years old with a family of her own, Moceanu recounts her life as a gymnast in an honest and interesting account of her family, her Olympic dreams, and the intense competition and sacrifice of a girl who began her training when she was 3 years old. Candid, strong, and beautiful, Moceanu weaves a tale through her childhood, the Olympics, and her life after gymnastics. Readers interested in the sacrifice and drive required of gymnasts and figure skaters should also read *Little Girls in Pretty Boxes* (1995) by Joan Ryan.

Mullen, P. H.
Gold in the Water: The True Story of Ordinary Men and Their Extraordinary Dream of Olympic Glory. 2003 (2001). St. Martin's Reprint Edition, ISBN 9780312311162. 352p.

The quest to be an Olympic swimmer is a daunting task, requiring years of rigorous training and personal sacrifice. Mullen chronicles the struggles, failures, and triumphs of several members of the Santa Clara Swim Club as they aim for the 2000 Olympics in Sydney, Australia. ★

Tevis, Walter
■ *The Hustler.* 2002 (1959). Thunder's Mouth Press, ISBN 9781560254737. 224p.

"Fast Eddie" Felson was immortalized on the silver screen by Paul Newman in 1961 and the story remains a prime example of great talent and bad decisions. Not a long book, Tevis excels at tight, emotional prose that conveys what it means to win, lose, and live. ★

For the Love of the Game (Not the Money)

Some people love the sport they play and would gladly play it without being paid. Other folks go out on the weekends and play golf, run, play softball just for the fun. Here are some books that reflect the joy of sports rather than the pay off.

Araton, Harvey
Alive and Kicking: When Soccer Moms Take the Field and Change Their Lives Forever. 2007 (2001). Simon and Schuster, ISBN 9781416575177. 256p.

An unlikely consequence of Title IX, a group of soccer moms formed their own soccer league in 1988 after missing out on sports during their youth. Araton's wife on being chosen for a team states, "no one's ever asked me to be on a team before." This is a story of camaraderie in sport as these women create a bond through soccer that helps them share life's problems and successes. ★

Feinstein, John
▶ *The Last Amateurs: Playing for Glory and Honor in Division I College Basketball.* 2001 (2000). Back Bay Books, ISBN 9780316278423. 480p.

Feinstein spends a season with the young men who play for Bucknell, Fordham, Lehigh, and others in a small conference of basketball. Their love of the game is fierce and they play without the prospect of an NBA future or televised fame. Interviews with players, coaches, and administrators convey a passion for basketball and amateur sport at its best. ★

Grisham, John
Playing for Pizza. 2007. Doubleday, ISBN 9780385525008. 262p.

Star quarterback Rick Dockery finds himself in the position of possible hero but turns into a goat as he throws three interceptions and single handedly dashes the hopes of Cleveland Browns fans (cliché?). He finds redemption and self-revelation in Italy as his agent lands him a job as quarterback for the Parma Panthers—in Italy. Football, food, and fiction make for a great combination.

Haner, Jim
Soccerhead: An Accidental Journey into the Heart of the American Game. 2007 (2006). North Point Press, ISBN 9780865477339. 288p.

The Baltimore Sun journalist Haner chronicles the excitement and spectacle of nine year olds playing soccer. He becomes the coach of his son's team and while researching ways to be a better coach, he relates a wonderful story of soccer history in the United States. The recent surge in the popularity of soccer is nothing new he writes, but has its origins in the immigration boom of the early 20th century. ★

Oxenham, Gwendolyn
🎬 *Finding the Game: Three Years, Twenty-Five Countries, and the Search for Pickup Soccer.* 2012. St. Martin's Press, ISBN 9781250002044. 304p.

A soccer player at Duke and almost pro, Oxenham wanted to write books and she wanted to play soccer, so she garnered a writing grant and traveled the world to do just that. Full of evocative settings and confident prose, she plays games on a rooftop in Tokyo, a prison in Mexico, and in the wondrous heat of Nairobi. Be sure to catch her documentary *Pelada*, which brings her travels to the screen.

Rea, Stephen
Finn McCool's Football Club: The Birth, Death, and Resurrection of a Pub Soccer Team in the City of the Dead. 2009. Pelican Publishing, ISBN 9781589806412. 336p.

Tired of playing pickup soccer, Irish expat Rea relents and joins up with the pub soccer team at Finn McCool's in New Orleans. Eccentric and amusing characters fill the team and to their surprise, they play quite well. Hurricane Katrina upends the team, but the group at Finn McCool's come together once again in a testament to the resilient nature of the folks from New Orleans. Touchingly sad and at times extremely funny, Rea's writing skills bring this story to life.

St. Amant, Mark
Just Kick It: Tales of an Underdog, Over-Age, Out-of-Place Semi-Pro Football Player. 2006. Scribner, ISBN 9780743286756. 256p.

Fantasy football writer and mediocre high school soccer player decides to find the glory of the game by becoming the kicker for The Boston Panthers, a semipro team in Boston. He finds himself immersed in the positive forces of the team mentality and he writes about his fellow teammates with humor, friendship, and respect. ★

Love and Devotion—Beyond the Games

On the field, professional athletes provide grand entertainment that inspires young and old to emulate them on playgrounds, high schools, and courts everywhere. These authors hope to inspire in a different way. Their lives have taken unexpected turns and tragedy or revelation, the game no longer matters. There are much more important things in life.

Ashe, Arthur and Arnold Rampersad
▶ *Days of Grace: A Memoir.* 1993. Knopf, ISBN 9780679423966. 317p. Y A
While Ashe recounts parts of his childhood, this thought-provoking and poignant memoir focuses on his post-tennis life after contracting AIDS during a blood transfusion. He became an advocate for others who suffered from AIDS, injustice in Africa, and the plight of Haitians entering the United States. Always a gentleman and philanthropist, Ashe spoke for those who had no voice.

Bissinger, Buzz
Father's Day: A Journey into the Mind and Heart of My Extraordinary Son. 2012. Houghton Mifflin Harcourt, ISBN 9780547816562. 256p.
The author of *Friday Night Lights* turns his pen inward as he writes about life with one of his twin sons Zach, who is a savant. The story follows Zach and Buzz on a cross-country trip in order to "unravel the mystery" that is his son. Part memoir, part confessional, and part revelation, Bissinger writes poignantly and personally about a journey of discovery.

Deford, Frank
▰ *Alex: The Life of a Child.* 1997 (1983). Rutledge Hill Press, ISBN 9781558535527. 228p.
NPR's voice of sports, *Sports Illustrated* writer for more than 50 years, and author of 16 books, Deford is a literary sports icon. In 1980, his daughter of eight years succumbed to cystic fibrosis. He lovingly describes the spirit and precociousness of Alexandra and you can feel his pain as he witnesses the suffering of his little girl. Deford was director of The Cystic Fibrosis Foundation until 1999.

Kelly, Jill
Without a Word: How a Boy's Unspoken Love Changed Everything. 2010. FaithWords, ISBN 9780446563376. 253p.
Wife of famed Buffalo Bills quarterback Jim Kelly writes about the couple's son Hunter, who was diagnosed with Krabbe disease in 1997 and

passed away in 2005 at age eight. Their faith kept them strong and Jill shares the feelings, suffering, heartbreak, and redemption that comes with the loss of a child.

Payton, Walter and Don Yaeger
Never Die Easy: The Autobiography of Walter Payton. 2000. Villard, ISBN 9780679463313. 288p.

Payton died of liver cancer shortly before the publication of this book; so Yaeger included interviews and statements from friends, family, and teammates and interspersed them throughout. One of the most celebrated and beloved players to grace the NFL, Payton was a true role model. Humble, loyal, and giving, Payton was an advocate for organ donation even though he could not receive a transplant.

Petrick, Ben
40,000 to One. 2012. KMP Enterprises, ISBN 9780615583457. 188p.

Petrick was the starting catcher for the Colorado Rockies from 1999 to 2002. After his retirement in 2004, he revealed that he was diagnosed with Parkinson's disease in 1999. He is now a father and a coach, and works to raise awareness for those who have Parkinson's. Honest, inspirational, and a firsthand account of a man who understands what is important in life: http://www.faithinthegame.tumblr.com/.

Spielman, Chris and Bruce Hooley
That's Why I'm Here: The Chris and Stephanie Spielman Story. 2012. Zondervan, ISBN 9780310336143. 224p.

Known for his hard-hitting tackles and intense on-field personality, Spielman was an All-American linebacker for Ohio State University and a four-time Pro-Bowler for the Detroit Lions. His purpose in life drastically changed in 2001 when his wife was diagnosed with breast cancer and succumbed to the disease in 2009. Stefanie and Chris fought breast cancer together, and Chris and his family continue the fight in Stefanie's name raising over 10 million dollars for research (Stefanie Spielman Fund for Breast Cancer Research).

Tillman, Marie
The Letter: My Journey through Love, Loss, and Life. 2012. Grand Central Pub., ISBN 9780446571456. 255p.

Pat Tillman suspended his NFL football career to enlist in the Army shortly after the 9/11 attacks. Sadly, he was killed in Afghanistan in 2004. His wife, Marie, shares Pat's "just in case" letter with readers and writes of her grief, sadness, and ultimate rediscovering herself through The Pat Tillman Foundation, which promotes leadership through scholarship to veterans: www.pattillmanfoundation.org.

I Can Do Anything You Can Do—Athletes with Disabilities

Athletes hindered by physical limitations seldom make it to the professional ranks in sports. These athletes, however, let nothing stand in their way of competing and excelling at professional or Olympic levels. They inspire others by putting to words their perseverance, dedication, skill, and struggles as they strive to reach the pinnacle of their games. Their stories run the gamut of humor and disappointment, setback and success, and most importantly they often pay tribute to those who encouraged them along the way.

Abbott, Jim and Tim Brown
Imperfect: An Improbable Life. 2012. Ballantine Books, ISBN 9780345523259. 304p.

> Born without a right hand, Abbott just wanted to play baseball. Well, a gold medal in the Olympics, a 10-year professional career, and a no-hitter isn't too bad for a guy who used to hide his wrist in his pocket. Told with wit, warmth, and humor, Abbott recounts his life from growing up in Flint, Michigan, to being a role model for disabled youngsters everywhere.

Allred, Lance
Longshot: The Adventures of a Deaf Fundamentalist Mormon Kid and His Journey to the NBA. 2012. HarperOne, ISBN 9780061718588. 250p.

> The fascinating part of this story is not the fact that Allred played three games for the Cleveland Cavaliers in 2008; it's the journey of growing up in a polygamy commune in Montana, struggling with obsessive-compulsive disorder, and being hearing impaired. He didn't play organized basketball until he was in eighth grade and he played collegiately for Utah and Weber State. Allred has a gift for writing as well, and he tells his story with wit, gracefulness, and an abundance of humor.

Hamilton, Bethany, et al.
🎬 *Soul Surfer: A True Story of Faith, Family, and Fighting Back to Get Back on Board*. 2012 (2004). MTV Books, ISBN 9781451679137. 304p. [Y][A]

> Bethany was a 14-year-old professional surfer when she lost her arm to a tiger shark attack. Back on her board less than a month after the attack, she recounts her harrowing accident, recovery, and ultimate triumph as her family, friends, and faith helped her continue to do what she loves. Written for a YA audience and made into a major motion picture.

Robles, Anthony
Unstoppable: From Underdog to Undefeated: How I Became a Champion. 2012. Gotham, ISBN 9781592407774. 224p.

Three-time All-American and 2011 NCAA wrestling champion, Robles takes readers on an inspiring journey of dedication, perseverance, and excellence. Born without a right leg, Robles begins wrestling during his freshman year in high school and with the support of his family, coaches, and mentors, he achieves greatness. Especially poignant is Roble's conversations about his mother's unflinching support of her unique and especially gifted son.

Runyan, Marla and Sally Jenkins
No Finish Line. 2002 (2001). Berkley Trade, ISBN 9780425186145. 320p.
Runyan was the first legally blind athlete to compete in the Olympics (1,500 m), and she has filled her trophy case with Paralympic Games medals and other world-class running awards. Runyan describes her challenges growing up with Stargardt disease using an elegant and humorous style as she strives for excellence not only in running but also in everything she does. A strong spirit whose biggest obstacle was sometimes herself, Runyan's story will inspire and entertain readers with both her challenges and her triumphs.

Scdoris, Rachel and Rick Steiber
No End In Sight: My Life as a Blind Iditarod Racer. (2006) 2007. St. Martin's Griffin, ISBN 9780312364373. 288p. [Y][A]
Legally blind since birth, Scdoris has let nothing stop her in school, athletics, life, and especially dogsled racing. In 2005, she became the youngest person to participate in the Iditarod, and in the 2007 edition, she adds a chapter on her 2006 race. Filled with tales of her childhood, being bullied in school, caring for dogs, and her beginnings in racing, Scdoris proves that if you believe in yourself and work hard, your dreams may come true.

Zupan, Mark
◼ *GIMP: When Life Deals You a Crappy Hand, You Can Fold—Or You Can Play.* 2006. Harper, ISBN 9780061127687. 288p.
The star of the acclaimed documentary *Murderball*, Zupan lives his life with vigor despite losing the use of his legs in a truck accident. More than a look into the world of Paralympic Rugby, Zupan speaks candidly about recovery, philosophy on living, and his attempts to not let his wheelchair constrain him from enjoying life. A bit explicit and irreverent at times, but also humorous and thoughtful.

Extraordinary Friendships

For many people, participation in athletics at any level yields friendships that last a lifetime. High school or college teammates spend years together, win or lose, and playing and practicing together help form long-lasting relationships. After years of competing against one another, some rivals become friends as they realize the common bond of their endeavors. We explore some exceptional friendships here as they provide fascinating stories of how they came together.

Bird, Larry, Earvin Johnson Jr., and Jackie MacMullan
When the Game Was Ours. 2009. Houghton Mifflin Harcourt, ISBN 9780547225470. 352p.

Every generation has its heroes and rivals, but for folks born around 1970 or before, Johnson/Bird was a sight to behold. From the 1979 NCAA championships through a decade of pro basketball, they put on quite a show winning seven NBA titles in the 1980s. Years of competition created a surprising by-product: in addition to the mutual respect they have for one another, they became friends.

Howard, Johnette
The Rivals: Chris Evert vs. Martina Navratilova Their Epic Duels and Extraordinary Friendship. 2006 (2005). Three Rivers Press, ISBN 9780767918855. 304p.

Their demeanor and appearance on the court could not have been more different: Evert a ponytailed blond from the Midwest, and Navratilova a serious and striking Czech. They played each other 80 times and more often than not they were facing each other in the finals. Howard examines each player during their reign over women's tennis, detailing their lives on and off the court. Theirs is one of the truly great rivalries in sport.

Kindred, Dave
Sound and Fury: Two Powerful Lives, One Fateful Friendship. 2007 (2006). Free Press, ISBN 9780743262125. 384p.

The 1960s and 1970s were an exciting and tumultuous time for sports. Televised sports were becoming the standard and few voices resonated like Howard Cosell's nasal timbre. Muhammad Ali shook the boxing world with his fighting skills and his penchant for verbal assaults as well. Cosell and Ali made for great television, driven by Ali's verbal jabs and Cosell's unflinching and candid questions. Kindred delves into the public and private worlds of these two great men who became friends.

Russell, Bill and Alan Steinberg
Red and Me: My Coach, My Lifelong Friend. 2009. Harper, ISBN 9781615537051. 208p.

Russell writes an homage to his coach and friend Red Auerbach. Together they were one of the greatest basketball dynasties of all time. Russell writes of his childhood and how his growing up amid segregation and prejudice allowed him to better understand this outwardly gruff Jewish man from Brooklyn. Russell reveals Red's humorous and generous side and entertains with his candor and engaging writing.

Stanton, Tom

Ty and The Babe: Baseball's Fiercest Rivals: A Surprising Friendship and the 1941 Has-Beens Golf Championship. 2007. St. Martin's Press, ISBN 9780312361594. 290p.

> These 2 giants of baseball battled against each other over 14 seasons. Almost the perfect opposites—Cobb small, conservative, and a base hitter, and Ruth a giant in all respects, these two mellowed over time and developed a respect and friendship after their playing days. Stanton represents both players' stories and brings them together at a golf match held shortly after their induction into Cooperstown. ★

Tschetter, Kris and Steve Eubanks

Mr. Hogan, the Man I Knew: An LPGA Player Looks Back on an Amazing Friendship and Lessons She Learned from Golf's Greatest Legend. 2011 (2010). Gotham Books, ISBN 9781592406715. 221p.

> It's a good thing she ignored the rule of not talking to Mr. Hogan, or Tschetter wouldn't have been able to write this tender and heartwarming ode to her friend and mentor Paul Hogan. From golf lessons to personal stories, this slim volume reveals some great details about a legendary golfer who was sometimes misunderstood.

It's Tebow Time—You Gotta Have Faith

Athletes express their faith in many ways. Tim Tebow spurred the online craze of "Tebowing," where people across the nation imitated his pose and posted pictures and videos on the Web. Throughout the history of sports, faith plays a great role for some athletes and manifests itself in many ways.

Ali, Muhammad and Hana Yaseem

The Soul of a Butterfly: Reflections on Life's Journey. 2010. Simon and Schuster, ISBN 9780743255691. 256p.

> Witness one of the greatest boxers of the 20th century as he shares his thoughts on his life in boxing and his growth spiritually. Told in a series of short essays, poetry, and Sufi parables, Ali conveys his unflappable faith and the beauty that emanates from his beliefs. Ali and Yaseem, his daughter, provide an intimate glimpse into a beloved man.

Buder, Sister Madonna and Karin Evans

The Grace to Race: The Wisdom and Inspiration of the 80 Year Old World Championship Triathlete Known as the Iron Nun. 2010. Simon and Schuster, ISBN 9781439177488. 256p.

> Buder knew she wanted to devote her life to God at a very young age and entered the convent in 1953. A priest, Father John Topol, introduced her to the mental, physical, and spiritual benefits of running and she has run countless

miles since that time. The "Iron Nun" doesn't know what all the fuss is about; she just likes to run triathlons and she trains "religiously." Uplifting, humorous, and full of spiritual joy.

Crothers, Tim

The Queen of Katwe: A Story of Life, Chess, and One Extraordinary Girl's Dream of Becoming a Grandmaster. 2012. Scribner, ISBN 9781451657814. 240p. Y A

Born into one of the worst slums in Uganda, Phiona Mutesi discovered the world of chess at a missionary outreach center called the Sports Outreach Institute. Prospects are dim for a teenage girl in Uganda, but Phiona developed an aptitude for chess that allowed her to travel to Siberia for the Chess Olympiad. A role model for hope, this story examines the essence of faith, hope, and determination. Expanded from an *ESPN The Magazine* article. ★

Hamilton, Josh

Beyond Belief: Finding the Strength to Come Back. 2010 (2008). FaithWords, ISBN 9781599951607. 288p.

Hamilton had a gift from God in his ability to play baseball. He excelled in his young years and was drafted at age 18, but his career was derailed by injury and drug addiction. Faith and family proved the cure he needed to turn him around and return to the game he loves. This reprint edition contains updates on Hamilton's life in 2010, although he has since left the Rangers and plays for Los Angeles today.

Johnson, Shawn

Winning Balance: What I've Learned So Far about Love, Faith, and Living Your Dreams. 2012. Tynedale Momentum, ISBN 9781414380926. 280p.

Shawn Johnson, a standout Olympic gymnast, won four medals in the 2008 games, including one gold. The balance in the title refers to keeping things in perspective while enduring the daily grind of preparing to compete in the Olympics. Her book is a mix of Olympic memories and preparation, and life lessons that she has learned on the way to adulthood. Will appeal to gymnast fans as well as those looking for an inspirational story.

Morris, Jim and Joel Engel

The Rookie: Big-League Dreams from a Small Town Guy. 2002. Little, Brown and Company, ISBN 9780316591560. 288p.

The Milwaukee Brewers drafted him in 1982, but injuries hindered him from being successful. He did have success as a father, teacher, and coach in his West Texas town, and his players and family urged him to try again for his dream of playing professional baseball. Engel and Morris make a good writing team in this authentic and uplifting story.

Oher, Michael

I Beat the Odds: From Homelessness, to The Blind Side, and Beyond. 2011. Gotham, ISBN 9781592406128. 272p.

Currently a defensive tackle for the Baltimore Ravens, Oher's success did not come easily. He describes his path from an early life of foster homes devoid of affection to the kindness and support of his adoptive family, the Tuohy's. He also stresses the need to help needy children and speaks tenderly of the many letters he receives from youngsters and offers advice on how to help them. The movie *The Blind Side* was based partly on Michael Lewis's book: *The Blind Side: Evolution of a Game* (2006).

Olney, Buster
How Lucky Can You Be: The Story of Coach Don Meyer. 2010. ESPN, ISBN 9780345524119. 240p.

Meyer was a successful college basketball coach who amassed over 900 wins during his career. Unfortunately, the rest of his life seemed to suffer due to his singular focus. In 2008, however, all that changed. Meyer had his leg amputated due to an accident and was diagnosed with cancer at the same time. His coaching career continued, but his focus changed to what he called his "f" words: faith, family, and friends.

Tebow, Tim and Nathan Whitaker
▶ *Through My Eyes.* 2011. Harper, ISBN 9780062007285. 272p. [Y][A]

He was the first sophomore to win the Heisman trophy, and he helped the Florida Gators win two NCAA championships, but what drives Tim Tebow to success is his much-publicized faith in God. The son of missionaries, Tebow delivers a passionate accounting of his life growing up with faith, the troubles and successes, and his hope for the future.

The Futility of Being a Cleveland Sports Fan (or How We Stopped Worrying and Learned to Love Defeat and Despair)

It has been a rough 59 years for Cleveland sports fans since the Cleveland Browns won an NFL championship in 1964. The Indians have not won a World Series since 1948. The Cavaliers have played just once in an NBA final (getting swept 4–0 by the San Antonio Spurs). And the Browns have never been to the Super Bowl. I know the Cubs haven't won a title since 1908, but the Bulls, Blackhawks, Bears, and White Sox have. San Diego also has a long drought, as do the Buffalo Bills who lost four Super Bowls in a row, some in excruciating fashion. We are not here to diminish any other city's suffering, only to revel in our own. "The Catch," "The Drive," "The Fumble," "The Shot," "Game Seven," and "The Decision": read about these fateful plays and more in the books on this list, though we would seriously advise not reading them all consecutively.

Knight, Jonathon
Sundays in the Pound: The Heroics and Heartbreak of the 1985–89 Cleveland Browns. 2006. Kent State University Press, ISBN 9780873388665. 313p.

Although they last won a NFL championship in 1964, the Cleveland Browns have had a bit of success over the intervening years. They were particularly strong from the mid to late 1980s. Led by Youngstown-born quarterback Bernie Kosar, these Browns were a playoff team in 1985–1989, losing to the Denver Broncos in heartbreaking fashion in 1986, 1987, and 1989. Knight's book takes us through those heady years and revisits the players that made them so memorable.

Long, Tim
Curses! Why Cleveland Sports Fans Deserve to Be Miserable: A Lifetime of Tough Luck, Bad Breaks, Goofs, Gaffes, and Blunders. 2005. Gray & Co., ISBN 9781598510188. 140p.

Long's book chronicles the misery he has encountered during his life as a Cleveland sports fan. It is a sad tale that details all the obstacles that have conspired to keep the long-suffering local sports fan from enjoying that most privileged of moments: a championship. He painfully recounts the lousy trades, misinformed draft picks, and sometimes rotten luck that has occurred in his lifetime.

Pluto, Terry
The Curse of Rocky Colavito: A Loving Look at a Thirty-Year Slump. 2007 (1994). Gray & Company, ISBN 9781598510355. 303p.

Growing up a Cleveland Indians fan in the 1960s was not a pleasant experience, and it didn't get any better through the 1970s and 1980s. Lots of trades and promises of better days ahead never seemed to bear fruit. Some believe all this started when slugger and beloved outfielder Rocky Colavito was traded in 1960. Pluto shows us that instead of a curse, the decades of ineptitude can be attributed to incompetent management. And maybe some bad luck also, as Pluto profiles 1960s pitcher "Sudden" Sam McDowell, who liked to drink as much as pitch, and 1970s slugger Tony Horton whose career was derailed by a bout of depression. Not for the faint of heart but of interest to any baseball fan, if only to make them feel good about their own teams.

Polk, Mike, Jr.
Damn Right I'm from Cleveland: Your Guide to Makin' It in America's 47th Biggest City. 2012. Gray & Company Publishers, ISBN 9781938441073. 108p.

Polk is a Cleveland-based comedian who has scored major hits nationally with his Internet videos, most notably "Cleveland Browns: Factory of Sadness." This book takes potshots at our favorite city, making fun of our hapless sports teams and constant attempts to become relevant again. A short but sour book that will appeal to a broad audience.

Raab, Scott

The Whore of Akron. 2012. Harper, ISBN 9780062066367. 302p.

When LeBron James left the Cleveland Cavaliers after the 2010 season (as a free agent), he did so in a manner that left the team in ruins. He incurred the wrath of not only Cleveland fans but also sports fans all over the country. Long-suffering Clevelander Raab had been following James throughout his "decision" year, and when James announced he was leaving the Cavaliers on national television, Raab didn't take it well. He turns his disdain for James and devotion to Cleveland into an examination of his own longtime battle with drugs and alcohol, family dysfunction, religious issues, and finally newly found happiness with his wife and son.

Sowell, Mike

The Pitch That Killed. 2003 (1989). Ivan R. Dee, ISBN 9781566635516. 352p.

Another "only in Cleveland" moment is splendidly presented by journalism professor Sowell as he recounts the tale of Ray Chapman, the only ballplayer ever to be killed by a pitched ball. The year was 1920 and Chapman was the shortstop for the Cleveland Indians. The opponent that day was the New York Yankees and their pitcher was Carl Mays. The story revolves around Chapman, Mays, and Joe Sewell, Chapman's replacement. The bigger picture has baseball going through many watershed moments including the Black Sox scandal and the Red Sox selling Babe Ruth to the Yankees. On the bright side, the Cleveland Indians won the World Series that year. Go figure. ★

Sources

We consulted a number of websites in order to compile titles, check biographical and bibliographic information, and research possible list categories. Those we used the most were Novelist, Amazon.com, Worldcat.org, Wikipedia.com, Kirkusreviews.com, LibraryThing.com, marylaine.com/bookbyte/sports.html, GoodReads.com, Booklist.com, and BleacherReport.com (Great lists for sport lovers). We also relied heavily on print copies of *Library Journal*, *Kirkus*, and *Booklist*.

"ASAMA: The American Sport Art Museum and Archives." *The American Sport Art Museum & Archives—Daphne, AL*. N.p., n.d. Web.

Carrigan, Henry L., Jr. "Defeat: Sports Books 2012." *PublishersWeekly.com*. N.p., September 28, 2012. Web.

Coffey, Michael. "The Sporting News."*Publishers Weekly*. June 25, 2012: 130. *Literature Research Center*. Web. July 6, 2012.

Dawidoff, Nicholas. "The Power and Glory of Sportswriting." Web log post. *Opinionator: The Power and Glory of Sportswriting. New York Times*, July 12, 2012. Web.

"History of Title IX." *TitleIX.info*. The MARGARET Fund of the National Women's Law Center, 2013. Web. July 21, 2013.

Layden, Tim. "CNNSI.com—SI For Women. *100 Greatest Female Athletes. Sports Illustrated*, n.d. Web. August 10, 2012.

LitLine. Some of the Best Literary Sports Books. www.litline.org/ABR/issues/Volume21/Issue3/literarysports.pdf&lrm.

Magee, C. M. "The Millions." *The Best Sports Journalism Ever (According to Bill Simmons)*. The Millions, October 12, 2008. Web.

McEntegart, Pete, L. J. Wertheim, Gene Menez, and Mark Bechtel. "CNNSI .com—*Sports Illustrated*—The Magazine—SI's Top 100 Sports Books of All Time—Sunday January 26, 2003 04:45 PM." *CNNSI.com—Sports Illustrated*. N.p., December 16, 2002. Web.

Mediatore Stover, Katie. "Art of the Pitch." *Novelist*. Ebscohost, 2009. Web.

"Olympics at Sports-Reference.com—Olympics Statistics and History." *Olympics at Sports—Football—Reference.com*. USA Today Sports Digital Properties, n.d. Web. June 27, 2013.

Ott, Bill. "Top 10 Sports Books." *Booklist*. September 1, 2009: 35. *Literature Research Center*. Web. July 6, 2012.

Ott, Bill (ed.). September 1, 2012. Spotlight on Sports [Special Section]. *Booklist*.

Pelletier, Joe. "Hockey Book Reviews.com: Classic Hockey Books." Web log post. *Hockey Book Reviews.com: Classic Hockey Books*. N.p., March 12, 2009. Web.

"Sports Biographies." *Bookmarks*, May–June 2009: no page. *Literature Research Center*. Web. July 6, 2012.

Wiedeman, Reeves. "Why Are Great Sports Novels Like 'The Art of Fielding' So Rare?" *The Atlantic*. N.p., September 26, 2011. Web.

Wiedeman, Reeves. "Why Can't Broadway Make a Good Sports Play?" The Sporting Scene. *The New Yorker*, 2012. Web.

Zimmerman, Greg. "The Cursed Dearth of Literary Sports Novels." *BOOK RIOT*. N.p., October 5, 2011. Web.

Books

We consulted many books in the <u>Read On</u> series and offer many thanks to those that went before us. Some other titles we used on our adventure include:

Crothers, Tim and John Garrity. *Greatest Athletes of the 20th Century*. Des Moines, IA: Sports Illustrated, 1999. Print.

Edgington, K., Thomas L. Erskine, and James Michael Welsh. *Encyclopedia of Sports Films*. Lanham, MD: Scarecrow, 2011. Print.

Kaplan, Ron. *501 Baseball Books Fans Must Read Before They Die*. Lincoln: University of Nebraska, 2013. Print.

Postman, Andrew and Larry Stone. *The Ultimate Book of Sports Lists*. New York: Black Dog & Leventhal Pub., 2003. Print.

Saricks, Joyce G. *The Readers' Advisory Guide to Genre Fiction*. Chicago: American Library Association, 2001. Print.

Schraufnagel, Noel. *The Baseball Novel: A History and Annotated Bibliography of Adult Fiction*. Jefferson, NC: McFarland & Co., 2008. Print.

Tuchman, Robert. *The 100 Sporting Events You Must See Live: An Insider's Guide to Creating the Sports Experience of a Lifetime*. Dallas, TX: BenBella, 2009. Print.

Wyatt, Neal. *The Readers' Advisory Guide to Nonfiction*. Chicago: American Library Association, 2007. Print.

Index—Titles by Sport

Name Index

Author names are provided in **Bold**.

157

About the Authors

CRAIG A. CLARK, MLS, Kent State University, has worked as a branch manager, circulation manager, and branch librarian for several Ohio libraries. Previous to becoming a librarian, he managed a local sporting goods store. Currently a stay-at-home-dad, Craig is a member of the RUSA CODES Reading List committee, which selects the best genre fiction for a given year in eight categories.

RICHARD T. FOX was a librarian at Cuyahoga County Public Library and Cleveland Public Library for close to 30 years. He is a past member of the RUSA CODES Sophie Brody medal committee for outstanding achievement in Jewish literature and former chair of the International IMPAC Dublin Literary Award for Cleveland Public Library. He has retired from librarianship, and when not working part-time, he is either reading or watching sports on TV.